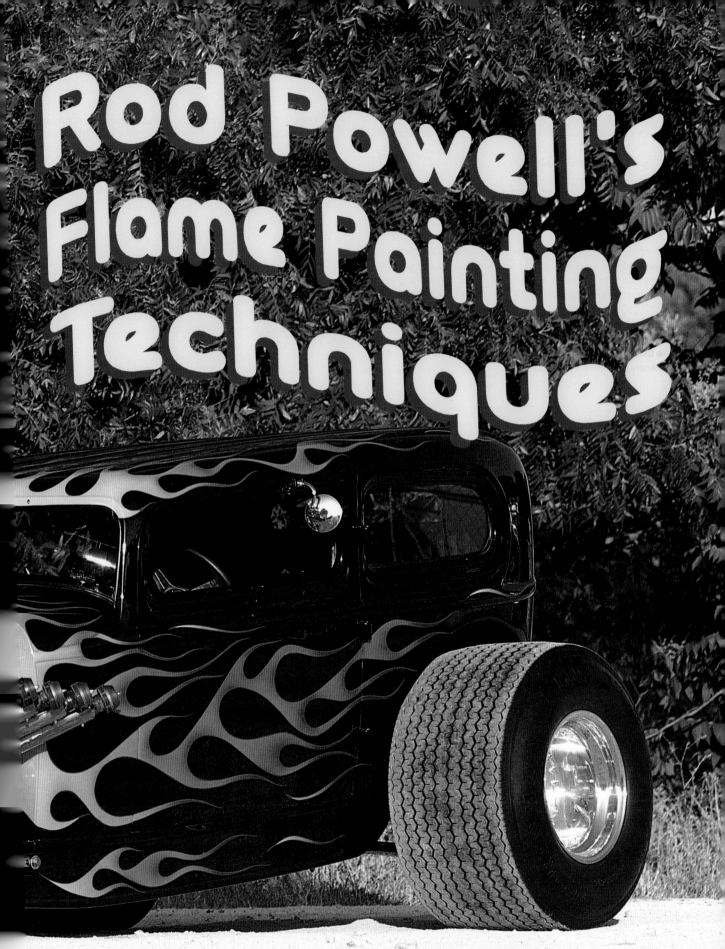

Rod Powell's Flame Painting Techniques

Rod Powell

First published in 1997 by Thaxton Press, PO Box 1742, Sebastopol, California. 95473 USA

The information in this book is true and complete to the best of our knowledge. All recommendations are made without any guarantee on the part of the author or Publisher, who also disclaim any liability incurred in connection with the use of this data or specific details.

We recognize that some words, model names and designations, for example, mentioned herein are the property of the trademark holder. We use them for identification purposes only. This is not an official publication.

Library of Congress Cataloging-in Publication Data Available
ISBN: 0-9652005-5-8

Printed in Hong Kong

Front Cover:
R.H. Jones had just created this track roadster kit car and wanted the first one to have a lot of impact. The Chrome Yellow bodywork really popped when I applied the red and orange flames. Once I was finished with my work, which took about two weeks, the car was taken back to the paint shop and clear coated. I then striped it at Jones' shop.

Frontispiece:
In this picture, taken about 1970, I am taping up Al Mendoza's '55 Nomad. This was a small shop and I painted the car exactly where you see it. The paint was acrylic lacquer and dried quickly. The base color was the new Murano Pearl that changed from black to blue and purple and the flames were colored in a transparent purple. We had seen a '57 Nomad with flames by Dennis Ricklefs and, while I didn't copy him precisely, the size of his flames and the way they continued into the doors and the 1/4 panels gave me inspiration for my work.

Back Cover:
John Rather called me from Minnesota and asked if I would do something, anything, striping and flames, on his grille cover as long as it included an eyeball. That was fine with me and this is the result. I was pleased with the design which used a lot of color although the bare aluminum was difficult to work over and smudge very easily. I recommend clear coating before, and after, applying the artwork. I used 1-Shot striping paint with a catalyst added. I used pre-mask paper and an airbrush to create the flames and the rest of the design was done with striping and lettering brushes.

Contents

Introduction

This book is intended to share with you photos, information, and techniques I've gathered over the past 40 years since I flamed my first car.

In the fifties, when I read the early articles on how to do custom paint work, the magazine pictures were out of sequence and there was little written information. Sometimes not even the same car was used for the whole article! In spite of these frustrations, I was fascinated by the designs and immediately tried to copy what I was seeing.

Because the creative part of flaming is what I find the most interesting, I recommend using this book as a guide to help in designing a flame job of your own. Every flame design is a unique creation and I have attempted here, with my own work and the works of others, to show color schemes, designs and techniques that will challenge your imagination.

I show what it was like when I began to paint flames in 1957 and how I do them today. I can't tell you how I will be flame painting tomorrow—I learn something new with every job.

Interestingly, even the process of writing and taking photographs, in preparation for this book, also opened my eyes to the possibilities of new ways of flaming.

It was not possible to list all the craftsmen who did the flames in this book but fortunately I have been able to document the outstanding work of some of them. If your work has been included in the following pages I hope you enjoy seeing it.

I have attempted to included the names of artists and car owners when the information was available but it was not possible to credit everyone. If I have included your work with no credit please accept my apologies and feel free to let me know.

This is not a book on how to paint cars, so I've haven't written much about paint materials. Rapidly changing regulations in many areas of the country dictate that any information given today may be obsolete

Acknowledgements

I would like to thank Dean Jeffries, Larry Watson, George Barris, Don Varner, Andy Southard, Dave Bell, Art Himsl, Von Franco, Greg Sharp and Tony Thacker for their help, information and photos for this book.

Technical projects like this book are never one man's work. These people and companies graciously helped me get it done: Creative Concepts, Western Auto Body, Espinosa's Auto Body and Lucky 7 Customs for the use of their facilities in the how-to portion of the book. I'd also like to thank Jon Kosmowski for his constant search for custom paint products that made much of this work possible, Gloria Fetherston for restructuring my notes and editing my text, and David Fetherston for his encouragement and support to put together this collection of photos, opinions, and information.

in a few months. There are many different brands of paint and materials available so I suggest you get to know the people at your local paint store and follow their advice. The larger car events across the country usually have automotive paint displays, and representatives are available there to answer your questions. Don't be afraid to ask questions and obtain all the information you can on the equipment and materials that you choose.

Flames are an easy place for a beginner to start custom painting; there are so many variations that no-one can say what is wrong or right. If the pictures shown here inspire you enough, grab a few rolls of 1/8th inch tape, and go for it! Take your time but don't expect to get it right with the first tape layout. You don't have to be perfect to have fun. If you're already painting use this book as a reference.

I get a lot of satisfaction from painting flames. They draw attention and magazine people have told me that a flamed car on the cover will usually generate extra sales of that particular issue.

Today, flames are everywhere, and not just on cars. Musical instruments, toys, clothing, works of art and fast food packaging are just a few of the many examples seen around us.

Keep on flaming and good luck with your future work.

Rod Powell
Sebastopol, California, 1997.

Publishers Acknowledgements:
Thaxton Press would also like to thank these wonderful folks: Gloria Fetherston for her skill in evolving and editing the manuscript, Teka Luttrell for his input on the design and layout, Paragon 3 in Santa Rosa, California, for their cover design work, and Nanette Simmons for her work on production.

Rod Powell's
Flame Painting Techniques

The Early Years

My father loved cars and when I was growing up in the fifties he took me to the hardtop races at the old Salinas Speedway every week. I remember going to the sports car races, too, at the Salinas Airport and in the forests around Pebble Beach. We always went to the Salinas Hi-Timer's drag races and it was exciting to see Garlits race at Kingdon on his first trip to California.

Above: This was dad's Cadillac-powered Lincoln. It was a hot rod in the true sense with its engine swap, black and white naugahyde interior and Kelsey-Hayes wire wheels

Dad had a '41 Lincoln with a Cadillac motor and his first new cars were the Hudson Hornets which were winning the stock car races in those days. When I was ready for a car he had just bought a new '56 Lincoln Premier two-door hardtop and wanted to give me his '51 Hudson or a '41 LaSalle coupe that he knew was for sale. I didn't want either of them, I had to have a '39 Chevrolet to fit in with the guys.

Someone else bought the LaSalle and all they did was lower it to make a really beautiful car and many is the time I've wished I had that LaSalle, or the Lincoln. I've been partial to big body styles ever since, and even though as a teenager I disliked Dad's Hudson four door, it would be a great car to have today.

As a teenager I was introduced to custom painting by way of the car magazines I kept hidden inside my school books. Mostly, I was interested in how the cars looked and reading about the people who owned and built them.

One of the advantages of living in California at

Above: This *Car Craft* issue featured the Barris-painted '29 roadster of Tom Pollard and the '32 "Flamer" coupe of George Sein.

that time was how often I could read about custom cars and hot rods in magazines and soon after see the real thing on the street or in a show. At the 1955 Monterey Kar Kapades the Barris-painted '29 roadster of Tom Pollard and the '32 "Flamer" coupe of George Sein appeared with their wild pinstripes, cartoon figures and unusual color combinations really grabbed my attention.

Naturally, all my friends were into cars and cars became our way of life. We started a car club called the "Road Runners" when I was a high school senior and I helped out putting on a car show. About that time I began drawing cartoons

Above: In 1958, some friends and I put on a car show in the football stadium. This picture shows Bob Travis outlining a flame-like design on Jim Smith's 1956 Ford custom. Bob was one of the guys who was striping in Salinas at the time. Whenever a striper was working, there would be a crowd around watching. As you can see by the bracket on the steering wheel and the plaque in the rear window, Jim was a member of the Coachmen car club.

and pictures of cars for my buddies and was soon striping the dashboards of their cars.

I would hang around any place there was a custom or a hot rod. I remember a friend's dad painted cars for us in his garage and he was the first guy I watched use a spray gun. My Saturdays were spent in wrecking yards getting parts while Sundays were for cruising around town or going to the drag races and car shows.

My first car was a completely original, light blue '39 Chevrolet Master Deluxe Tudor sedan. I borrowed $125 from my parents to pay for it and quickly removed the hood ornament with a hacksaw. That worked so well I decided to lower the front end, again using the hacksaw. Unfortunately, the lowering didn't go quite as easy as the hood ornament and I ended up having to get the coils melted by a friend who had access to a torch in the high school auto shop. I painted the wheels copper, the hot color that summer, with a spray can, installed big and little tires with Port-a-walls, spray-canned the dash gray primer and drew weird cartoons on it.

The Kookie Kar was an inspiration to me so I had to have a floor shift with a skull. Mine was so heavy it wouldn't stay in second gear, which was essential for dragging Main Street, so I tried an eight ball stolen from the Rodeo pool hall. It was still too heavy so I started making gearshift knobs in the plastic shop

Above: This is my first flame job on my '39 Chevy Sedan. I had already painted it in yellow primer and this shows the 1/4-inch tape design. The car was pulled out of the garage to check out before masking up.

Left: This is a finished photo of that first flame job. The flames were painted in lavender primer with white tips and it was very colorful as the wheels were still bright red. It was also my first attempt at nerf bars using an overrider I found at the junk yard.

and they worked a lot better.

My first custom work was when Lacey's Custom Shop louvered the hood for $18.00 and put it in primer before I pinstriped flames coming out of the louvers with red house paint. I bought a set of full length lakes pipes and had a friend prime the car in yellow so I would have a base for my first flame job. But that wasn't my first experience at custom painting though—that honor fell to a friend's '50 Ford which I scalloped, painted a large weird cartoon on the deck lid, and striped the dash. This work was all accomplished in the barn at his girlfriend's parents' ranch.

The next weekend I was back in the barn to flame my '39 Chevy. I did the layout at home in my parent's garage using 1/4-inch tape and newspapers, and my mother helped me by cutting circles out of newspaper to fill in the design. I think she wanted me to get done faster so that she could park the family car inside the garage again. Looking back, I realize how supportive my parents were of my early efforts.

After the car was masked up—leaving the windows clear, of course—I drove to the ranch where I sprayed the flames and was out dragging Main Street that afternoon. I can remember Don Varner coming towards me in his truck and turning to look as I drove by, and making somebody look was what it was all about for me. I was 16.

Not everything was self taught, however. Walt Karcich taught body and fender classes at Hartnell Junior College and he was very easy going. He allowed us to do custom work on our cars and some guys even built complete cars—hot rods, customs and dragsters—in class. Chopping, channeling and sectioning were common and everyone was trying to be a custom painter.

At first I painted in lacquer making my own colors with pearls and toners long before I ever sprayed a stock color. My second '39 Chevy was the first car I painted completely, in purple lacquer blended using one of Don Varner's formulas. I entered this car in the 1961 Oakland Roadster Show where my class had 20 cars competing

for three trophies. My reward was a dash plaque which meant as much to me then as getting an award.

My first job was working in a service station where I was allowed to work on my own car when we weren't busy. The station was located on a corner where everyone in Salinas cruised from the drive-ins on Main Street to Lacey's Custom Shop and Sal's Drive-In on the other side of town. There was a signal light at the intersection so I

Above: This was my second '39 Chevy and also my first complete paint job. It is seen here at the Oakland Roadster Show where I showed it with angel hair and Plymouth Fury hubcaps.

Right: This was my third '39 Chevy which had been painted in Yellow Pearl. It is shown here masked up, using newspaper, in preparation for its Candy Green flames.

was able to watch a lot of street racing if they were headed west. To the east were railroad tracks where the lowered cars had to come to a stop and would crawl slowly across. There were no hydraulics in those days and sometimes everyone but the driver had to get out of the car so they could get over the bumps in the road.

Eventually, I left the service station and started painting used cars for Douglas Samuels. He charged $39.00, bought all the materials and gave me $10.00. In a good week I could prep and paint a car a day and make $50.00 but the take home pay was only about $35.00. On top of this work I was custom painting at night school or at home in my garage.

My first notable flame job was done at home on Richard Bass' '40 which had already been re-paired by other body shops but needed to be smoothed up in a lot of areas before I could paint it. As I recall, it was winter time and I kept blowing fuses because of the heaters needed to keep warm. I finished it in black lacquer and Richard drove the car for a year while I tried to talk him into flames. Finally, he got the money together, about $125.00, and I painted the flames in my garage.

I wanted to do it like the '40 Ford coupe Von Dutch had done for Manuel Gonzales, but Richar wanted fatter flames. When it was done, Andy Southard striped it, photographed it and sent the article to *Rod & Custom* magazine. It appeared on the cover of the August, 1968, edition and it was the first flame job I ever had on a magazine cover. People really started noticing the '40 after

Above: This photo of my sectioned '39 shows how low this car was. I had great time with this car and people liked it. Dick Mendonca took this photo of me when he photographed it for *Rod & Custom*. I won "Readers Pick" with it from *Rod & Custom*.

...eft: I did the flames on this '40 ...oupe for Richard Bass. They ...ere patterned after Manual ...onzales' coupe, featured on the ...over of *Car Craft* with the Bob ...cCoy '40 Ford sedan. I made ...e flames much fatter and it ...rned out to be my first ...blished flame job when it ...ppeared on the cover of *Rod & ...ustom*.

...ght: The shape of flames on ... sectioned '39 Chevy were just ... I had originally wanted to put ... the coupe of Richard Bass. ...e flame combination in yellow ...d green was most unusual and ...ned out just as I wanted. It ...s my most requested color ...mbination for years after I ...shed it.

that and I began seeing other '40s in the magazines with the same pattern. I soon realized that it was a real compliment to have others like my work enough to want to copy it. After all, imitating Von Dutch, Jeffries and Watson was how I got started.

My second '39 Chevy sedan was also my first major custom and alot of people liked that car because it was sectioned and had other custom bodywork. I built it in 1969 to take to Andy's Picnic thinking that the body modifications would classify it as a custom car—I was wrong. The term "street rod" had just appeared on the scene and quickly became a generic term for an older, modified car. I didn't see any other cars that were sectioned and had rolled pans, nevertheless, they insisted on calling my car a street rod. It just goes to show how out of touch people were with customs by that time. They just didn't know what they were looking at.

Most people didn't know what had been done to my car so I like to think it was the sublety of my modifications, aside from the paint, which confused them. I wanted something different, something like candy yellow with flames in green or purple. I had seen Jim Noteboom's '32 painted green and yellow by Larry Watson and Barris' "The Chipmunk Car" with great pearl yellow

fenders and they inspired me. Also, I discovered Watson was using a new paint that changed colors. I had heard about Murano MYHP Gold Pearl so I bought a can to try out.

I began with a white base followed with bright yellow toner. Next, I mixed the pearl in clear and sprayed the brightest pearl yellow I've ever done. The car had lots of curved areas and highlighted from all angles. It looked like candy but I didn't use any transparent toners and after it was finished other painters would argue with me about how it was done. They all thought there was a secret to it and yet it was so easy—it was all luck!

After the car was painted yellow, everyone told me I would ruin it if I flamed it, especially in candy green. It was 1968 and some people thought flames were out of style. Flames are never out of style and it turned out to be one of my favorite paint jobs, holding its brightness and lasting for 16 years. It even won a few awards.

When I finally sold the car, the new owner repainted it in a monochromatic black with a green pearl tint. It was very nice but in my opinion, it just didn't stand out any more. In custom yellow with green flames, the car grabbed people's attention. The same paint job would have had just as much impact on a car that was lowered but with less body modifications.

Right: My '56 Chevrolet Wagon/ Delivery ready to paint. This was taken about 2:00 a.m. I was also flaming a friend's El Camino at the same time and he was helping. I remember wetting the floor and spraying them right out in the middle of the shop. The painting was finished around sunrise and I was unmasking them when my crew arrived for work that morning.

I worked for a number of different shops and id custom painting on the side until 1969 when I pened full time in a two-stall garage where it eems I always managed to cram in at least four ars. During the next 25 years, I created all kinds f show and custom cars for customers. However, did take the time to create some special customs r myself. For example, I had a '56 Chevy station agon which my painter, Jack Bradford, had rayed in black lacquer. Everyone said, "It looks good, don't flame it, you'll ruin it!" I flamed it yway and the flames were everything I wanted em to be. Alan Smith lettered it for me and it as a great advertisement.

took a lot of time making sure that the designs l not match side for side. They were completely different but the balance and flow was so close that very few people noticed. However, I would catch other painters pointing out how I didn't get it the same on both sides. The ones who understood knew what I was doing. The flames gave the car an attitude that kept it out of the street machine category for a while.

It was such a neat car and I enjoyed driving it in the early morning and seeing the flames flicker into life with the sunrise through the chopped windshield. It turned out to be one of the most enjoyable cars I've built for myself during those 25 years and it's one car I would like to own again. I sold the car to Boyd Coddington and it changed hands a number of times after that and like the '39 it was repainted with a monochromatic color and refined to perfection. I heard that the artist David Mann owned it for a while. He did a painting of it for Easyrider magazine.

The Beginnings of Flaming

Although flame painting was called just "a fad" when it first appeared in the magazines of the fifties, it has evolved into many forms. While many other styles of custom painting, such as graphics, scallops, panel painting and lace painting, have come and gone, flames have endured and remained popular, almost unchanged, through the years.

It's impossible to say with any certainty who painted the first set of flames but it's probably safe to say that they evolved onto race cars from the scallops painted on post-World War 1 airplanes.

When I interviewed some

Above: Many early Indy cars had flames but I think that they may have first appeared on race cars at the small speedways around the country from the thirties onward. The cream and blue "Spike Jones Special" started third on the grid in the 1946 Indy 500.

Below: This little flamed midget was raced by Australian Frank "Satan" Brewer in the late forties. Frank is pictured here behind the wheel, before a race at Saugas, California.

Left: The famous George Barris flamed Ford station wagon appeared on the cover of *Rod & Custom* Magazine in March, 1955. Here we see it being pinstriped by Von Dutch. Note the rough taped edges which Dutch is covering with a broad pinstripe. (See page 107.)

Below: Dean Jeffries and his girl friend Carol Lewis brought her new '56 Chevrolet to the Monterey Kar Kapades. These cars were still in the dealer's showrooms at the time and it was quite impressive to see something like this. In California at that time new cars were quite popular and with a few custom touches such as lowering, custom hubcaps and wild paint designs you would be ready for the show circuit.

ainters of the fifties they told me that although hey'd tried to paint cars to look like they were n fire, Von Dutch was the first who came up vith designs which, even though they didn't ook exactly like fire, captured its essence. The atterns that so obviously emanated from those rst Von Dutch efforts have become a part of ur culture and are now visible everywhere in dvertising, clothing, fast food packaging and l other forms of art.

The one time I met Von Dutch, he told me he dn't paint cars and was very firm about that. ut, if Von Dutch wasn't the first custom inter, who was? Custom paint spread from alifornia because it was easy to imitate but the terviews I conducted revealed that Dean ffries was probably the first artist to do a mplete paint job, start to finish. "Jeff," as he as known, was capable of laying out the sign, spraying the paint and then finishing th pinstripes and or lettering and cartoons.

Above: I love this photo of Carol Lewis showing her surprise at the Jeffries' flame job on her 1956 Chevrolet. It was great work like this that set the trend for the future of flamed cars. Photo: G Barris.

I know that "Dutch" was the first to stripe an outline around a flame design and he was the first to create what I now call "hot rod flames." Although there are other flame designs that have influenced today's styles including oriental, sacred, and tattoo art, I feel everything was developed from those first early Von Dutch examples.

In no time, another bright flame, Larry Watson, was giving him a lot of competition. Inevitably, the ranks began to swell and eventually there were many capable painters doing candy colors and two-color paint.

However, the ones who used tape layouts, striping, and lots of color in their work were the real custom painters in my opinion. They had the artistic ability and style which set them apart from the rest. Today, many competent painters who follow the technical information and use the right equipment and material can do work that, before, only a custom painter used be able to accomplish.

Stripe Time

When I wanted to learn more about striping I read about it in magazines and watched stripers at the car shows. The early articles on Von Dutch and Dean Jeffries didn't give much information about how to actually do the work. There were pictures of finished designs that seemed like something only highly talented people could do and I was left with the impression that you had to be an eccentric artist to pinstripe.

It also helped to be a comedian or an entertainer who could work in front of people. Most of the stripers I saw back then had some kind of trademark such as funny hats, airbrushed sweat shirts or D.A. haircuts. They also had paint on their clothes and acted weird. Of course this attracted a crowd and I was always in that crowd watching for hours, hoping to learn more. Everyone who striped acted as if it was a big secret and very difficult. They took the labels off their paint cans and kept their brushes in special boxes so people couldn't see what they were using; they all had special formulas or a "secret ingredient" that was added to the paint that made it unique. When I started striping I acted the same way! I never did like working in front of people though, I preferred to work at home or, in later years, in my shop.

My first striping efforts were footprints walking out of the ash tray and around the top of the dashboard of my dad's Hudson. I used poster paint because my model airplane paint dried too fast. I soon discovered that Sherwin Williams' housepaint worked better than others and that I could buy Mack striping brushes at the auto parts store which were sold to touch up chips and scratches.

I had watched Jeffries striping at the Monterey Kar Kapades but, until I met Don Varner and saw him striping, I was self-taught. Don let me hang around and I watched him laying flames and scallops with tape and spraying candy colors. I wanted to learn to stripe like him and although he didn't actually teach me, he was friendly and answered my questions. I would return home to practice striping on my Chevy dashboard and other stuff, like fishing tackle boxes and cabinet doors. I remember my younger brother watching me—I came in the garage one day and he had striped our lawnmower!

I practiced on my own car because I didn't want to mess up someone else's. Eventually I gained enough confidence to work on my friend's cars and my early work was mostly cartoons on dashboards and decklids.

I had Don stripe my '39 Chevrolet coupe because I wanted some of his work. Just watching him do it taught me a little more. I remember when Don striped my car because that day I met Andy Southard who stopped by Don's house on one of his cross-country visits from New York.

He was driving his new '58 Impala already customized and sporting a set of scallops that were as nice as anything I'd seen done on the West Coast. Andy did a lot of magazine articles and was an expert at striping, scalloping, and panel painting as well as photography. He didn't do many flames but there's an example of his work on Page 111 showing a '40 Mercury on which he used striping brushes and enamel paint. When he moved to Salinas we became friends and he helped me by striping the edges of my flames and encouraging me to continue my own striping efforts.

Striping is one of the first things I encourage newcomers to custom painting to learn. The equipment and materials are minimal compared to other types of painting, and mistakes can be easily corrected.

It does take lots of practice and many painters give up after the first few efforts. Outlining my flames gave me a new experience and by the time I was through with the first one I had learned a lot. Most sign painters can stripe and the sign supply stores carry everything that's necessary to get started. Many auto paint stores also carry striping brushes and One-Shot striping enamel.

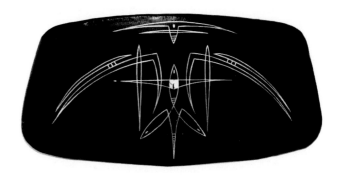

Above: This is an old glovebox lid I striped using traditional shapes and lines.

Rod's Flaming Philosophy

When I'm working on a flame design I try to feel relaxed and calm. Often, I'll pick up a pen and doodle designs on paper or any handy surface. I find that these drawings can often give me ideas that can be used.

My real design work comes when I get into the rhythm and motion of drawing out a design with 1/4-inch masking tape on the surface of a car. This is my favorite part of the whole process.

When I see flames on a car I seem to look at only the designs and colors, mostly ignoring the car itself. The body style of the car has a great deal to do with the way the design works out although the flames are, naturally, the main element. The art work is not just a detail and some of my best work occurs when the vehicle does not overpower my design.

The style of the vehicle also has a lot to do with its finished look. Harley-Davidsons and '40, '32, or '34 Ford hot rods are all recognized as classic candidates for flames; they take a design much better than a family sedan or most foreign cars. Volkswagen bugs seem to be an exception to this rule while commercial vehicles and even big-rig semi trucks are popular subjects for flaming.

Proper stance is also important. If the vehicle is lowered it helps enormously. I believe in "the lower, the better" but then I've never been too concerned with practicality.

Since flames are an automotive art form, their colors are determined by what is available from the automotive paint stores. Most of the new car finishes are done in tri-color (base-coat, color-coat, clear-coat). This is similar to what we used to call candy colors in the early days of custom painting.

Automotive paint manufacturers now have an entire array of custom paint colors that are variations of factory colors. The mystery has been taken from this important part of the custom car building process and it's now much easier to achieve good results. By using the proper equipment and materials, results can be very impressive. Many of today's body shops are producing work that only a "Kustom" painter could have done in the past.

A new hot rod or custom may look fantastic with a tri-color pearl from a Lexus or even a new Mustang candy apple red, but the uniqueness fades when seen alongside a new car or a van with the exact same color.

At this point a car owner may start thinking about how a paint design could help to personalize his car and his next step is to find someone to do the work and this is where the custom painter enters the scene.

Most people who want a custom paint job want to make a personal statement, to stand out and attract attention. Therefore, when I approach the job I try not to copy other people's work.

Occasionally, the customer has an idea of what they want in the form of drawings, pictures, or magazine articles and it helps me to see what they like or don't like about the flames they've seen.

Many designs I am shown stay away from the problem areas and therefore require less masking and clean up. This accelerates the work and reduces costs. On some cars it is worth the extra effort to go under the headers, off the frame rails or over the louvers.

A design aid I've used for years is a clipping file of flame photos, sketches, postcards, magazine articles, advertisements and scraps of paper. I refer to this often for inspiration.

I may draw some sketches after the work is in progress to help me visualize where I am headed. I find this especially helpful if I can't get the car outside the shop and step back to view it from a distance. People who see these sketches think I did them in advance to show me what to do, but I've usually figured out the design when I get to this stage.

When I begin a new flame job, I picture in my mind the base color as important as the flames themselves—it is significant to keep a balance or symmetry to this portion of the work. Sometimes, I see these areas as clusters of teardrops or tadpole shapes flowing toward the front of the vehicle, instead of flames streaming to the rear. I like to show curves and sensuous shapes that give movement and rhythm to the work, making the car look as if it is moving even while standing still

When I'm doing the taping I relax, it helps me develop new ideas and work out the difficult areas more easily. I like to design directly onto the car using 1/8-inch or 1/4-inch masking tape. This gives a smoother appearance to the curves, teardrop and looped areas. The tape shows clearly where the flame will be, making it easier to visualize the work in progress.

Most designs look their best from one or two

angles—the rear-3/4 angle or a full side view, seem to look best to me. When I stand back and look at a front-3/4 angle it makes the flames appear to be foreshortened and awkward. One of the reasons I don't rely on drawings is because they only show one or two angles and they aren't 3-dimensional.

When I am taping designs, I always do more than one. Even if I am pleased with the first version, I go to the opposite side and try something different. I then choose the one I like best. I might do this several times before I make my final decision.

It is not unusual for me to make changes in an almost finished design by removing major parts of the taping because I didn't like the way it was heading. This seems to be the way my creative process works at times but some of my best jobs visually have been quickies on a less-than perfect car, done just for fun.

When I am free of the strain of making everything perfect, I can relax and the design just seems to flow. It is also good to get away from the work for a while if I get stuck on a detail. Sometimes leaving it overnight helps and I will position the car so that the detail is the first thing I see when I walk in the next day. If I like what I see I am probably on the right track.

Flames appeared on race cars in the thirties following the tradition of adding sponsors' artwork and drivers' names. The evolution of these automobile graphics to hot rods was a natural. With the addition of pinstriping at the beginning of the fifties they became a hot rod art form. Flames have held their appeal and stayed in style much longer than any new fad graphics, however even a flame job won't help all cars.

Below: My friend Jimmie wanted his new truck done with "lots of flames." I made the patterns larger and bolder than I would on a smaller car because I wanted the design to accent the length of the truck body with flickers added on the rear fenders. Jimmie also bought a new trailer and decided it should match the truck. I called on Von Franco to airbrush a chrome style J. V. emblem along the raised body molding with a flying eyeball behind it. We also lettered it with the "Strange Pleasure" logo.

Flame Styles

When Von Dutch began striping and flame painting cars that were driven on the street, rather than on the race tracks, his efforts quickly attracted the attention of other talented individuals. Soon there was more than one painter that could do the work and they began to compete for customers. Each person developed his own style and followers, giving themselves interesting names like "Watson's seaweed flames" and "Roth's Crazy Painting." This practice of creating a personal style and labeling it with a distinctive title continues today. In this section of the book there are examples of different styles of flames and, as I found while researching these, there are more similarities than there are differences to the work. The names given them are for descriptive purposes only and are not the only ones that can be used for the particular designs that are shown.

One of the many purposes of this book is to have fun painting flames. Only a few of the variations of flame designs are shown here; you may also know of a dozen others that are equally impressive.

Below: The famous Von Dutch-flamed, Earle Bruce, Mercedes Benz "Gullwing." The Mercedes was a turning point in the history of flaming as not only did it look outrageous but it put a hot rod style on a foreign car to great effect. Dutch and Bruce were buddies and Dutch flamed the car because of an early candy paint job which was mottled around the lower section of the body. It is seen here at a Pomoma, California, race event in about 1955.

Color Variations

Unusual color combinations are not for everyone but combined with a good design they can be quite impressive. One way to attract attention to a car is to be different. A knowledge of color might be helpful to some people but there is also something to be said for the freedom of going against the flow due to the lack of knowledge or innocence of the established rules of color and design. If everyone used the same colors it would be just as boring as the monochromatic, single color paint of which we see so much.

Right: This is a great color scheme although it's not for everyone. The flames go right over the louvers and even down the smoothed and painted running boards. The body color on the front of the fenders looks like a panel design.

bove: Steve Warner has done nice job on his wife Debbie's 5 Chevrolet. Steve used aque colors for double flames ing them such a clean edge at striping wasn't necessary. e blue tips on the red make a ce contrast.

ght: Purple is a popular color d with the addition of some low flames it stands out more. te how the removal of the od side panels cause a break he pattern. If the sides are ng to be removed try to plan it when laying out the flames. e way the ends are continued the doors in this example is ood way to extend the design t the engine compartment. also have to be aware of things will look when the d panels are on.

Traditional Flames

Flame jobs on early hot rods were done as a visible sign of rebellion with bold and vibrant primary colors. The traditional or old style look is usually on a black car with red flames, sometimes blending into yellow, and no extra frills such as crossovers or extra flickers off the tips. Usually, the tips of the flames turned outward instead of inward and if they were outlined with a pinstripe, it was always done in white. Since they were on cars that were stripped down and speed was an important factor, the work didn't need to be perfect. In the late sixties and early seventies, more subtle blending of colors, for example, yellow into orange into red, began to be seen and the outline striping would sometimes be done in a medium blue. This later version is accepted by most flamers today.

Below: R.H Jones' '40 Ford is another traditionally flamed hot rod. Jones instructions said "Flame it!" So I did. It was done in 1993.

Below: This an excellent example of early style flames done by Tom "Itchy" Otis. On a classic black hi-boy he has used traditional colors of yellow into orange with white striping. The flames streaming off the hood and down the sides give it a very high speed look. The small peaks in the design around the louvers add a nice touch and show more imagination than a straight line. It is also a way to avoid working across the louvers which can be a real chore.

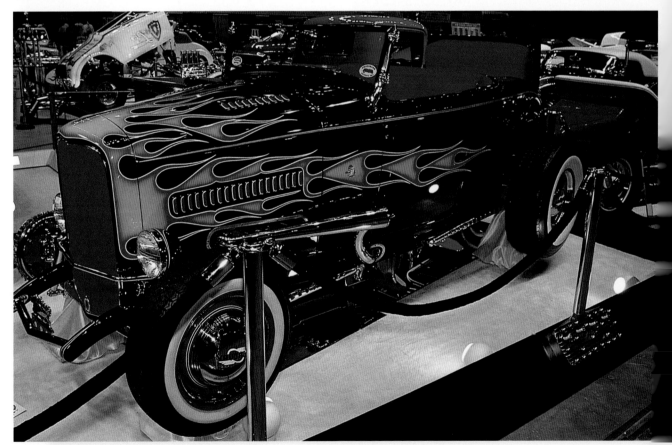

Asymmetrical Flames

Asymmetrical flames differ from side to side. They are often similar but definitely not the same. The asymmetrical style can eliminate the need for a pounce pattern, thus saving considerable time. A lot of people like these because symmetrical flames look "too" perfect. Both sides of a car can't be seen at the same time anyway. Most styles of flames can be used to create asymmetrical flame designs.

Below: The flames on this '34 Ford are completely different from side to side but most people have to look twice to see it. A very nice job with a good balance between the base color and the color of the flames. There is a lot of action in this flame job.

Primer Car Flames

Primered cars had a rebellious reputation and so did flames, and my favorite class in the early car shows was the unfinished custom class where the cars had colored primer, no interior and soaped windows. I thought it was a great look but that may have had something to do with the fact that I couldn't afford to paint my own cars!

Below: Eric Limone's Plymouth is a great example of primer, flames and scallops. The scallop designs are used to accent the lines of the car and they are an unusual choice for a full custom. Used to accent areas that might not show up with the dark primer, the scallops tie the body lines into the flames very nicely. This design was done by Alan Eglington, a cartoonist and underground comic artist.

Below: This is another fine flame design with wiggly scallops for accents on a primered car. Extra striping adds to the flame designs. Note the voodoo head striped on the front of the hood. There's no custom bodywork done to this car except for the Cadzilla style grille. The custom designs were done by the owner, Tommy Herrera, who also does great cartoon hot rod art work.

Crossover Tips

Crossover tips require more work but people really like them. They give an extra dimension to the flames and can make them appear to have depth, especially if they are highlighted at the crossover part. However, once the base color has been applied, everything becomes the same color and it is easy to overlook some of the crossovers. To keep track of them as I'm working, I count the crossovers on each panel, mark them on the car or make a quick sketch in a notebook. Matching the tips on each side at the same time also makes it easier to keep track of what you are doing.

Below: This is Jim Bushaw's '57 Ford Sedan Delivery. It was built by him during the time he was my shop manager. We flamed it in Candy Oriental Blue over silver with purple pinstriping. Jim specifically wanted overlapping tips on the flames and we worked together on the colors and shapes.

Crossover - Overlap Flames

With this style of flame the body of the flames go across each other. It also requires extra masking but it is not as much work as doing double flames.

Right: There is a lot of work in this Volkswagen. The flames go over the louvers and also the hidden headlights. The flames add a lot to the car by doing it this way. It is much more work masking and striping on the louvers.

Double or Overlay Designs

These are two sets of flames that have been applied one on top of the other. The patterns flow over and under each other and there are usually many crossovers making a lot of complicated work. If the edges are striped, things get even more confusing. These flames should be clear coated between designs to keep the edge from showing through the next set of flames. The layup goes like this: Apply base color, add flames, clear coat, sand, stripe, clear coat, sand, add second flames, clear coat, sand, stripe, clear coat, sand, buff to a shine.

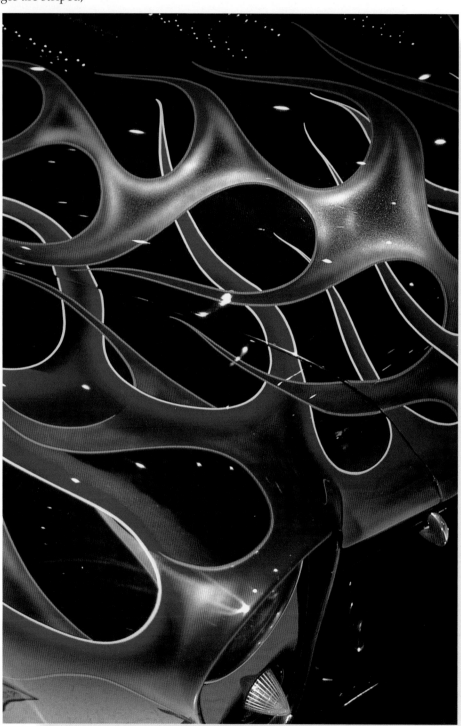

ght: There are so many flames here
s hard to tell if there is a car under
m. The multicolor red, pink and
ple designs twist and wrap around
h other for a very radical look.
ough there are only two sets of
nes it appears to have a lot more.

Pinstripe Flames

These are done by striping only the outline of the flame with a brush. The advantage is that there is no spraying involved and it is less expensive. This can be a very nice effect for a lot less money.

These two photos of pinstripe flames show both simplicity and complexity. The upper image is a simple pinstripe while the more complex design was done by Lil' Louie in two colors with many crossovers.

Pull-out Tape Flames

This is a style that can give a finished edge to a flame pattern without the use of a striping brush. The outline tape must be applied more carefully than with other types of flames. Try to use one length of tape from tip to tip because overlaps can show as bumps or glitches in the line. Carefully trim the ends of the tape to a point with a razor knife. After masking and painting the flames carefully remove all the tape except the original outline. At this point you can spray a light transparent shade of the flame color that will define the stripe when the tape is removed, or you can cover the flames and spray another color, leaving a bolder stripe. This was very popular in the seventies.

Below: This '40 Willys pickup was a drag car that I painted and flamed in the early seventies. It was painted with a gold powder base and tape striped using 1/8-inch masking tape which was brand new on the market. It was painted using Pagan Gold, Tangerine and Candy Red toners over a gold bronzing powder base and then highlighted with a light black shading for extra depth. There was no brush striping on this car.

Rainbow Flames and Striping

Using many shades of color to produce a rainbow effect will make a car stand out. It is a tricky technique that requires knowledge of the way the different colors blend when they are sprayed over each other, as well as a sense of design and proportion. Rainbow striping is done by striping with different brushloads of colors as the line progresses. This also calls for skillful use of the paint materials and advanced methods of pinstriping.

Below: This 1939 Ford was at an event in the mid-seventies. I believe the flames were done by "Yosemite Sam." Note the way the paint surrounds the windows and flows into flames at the rear of the roof sail panel. There is a lot of color in this one.

Right: Dave Bell did this '29 sedan showing streamer-like flames which go over the louvers. The flickers are also well done with fireballs. Note how the pinstriping is blended with many different colors, adding to the rod's unique look.

3-D Flames

This is tricky but it gives a three dimensional look to the flames that many people enjoy. Drawing out these designs to see how the patterns will be emphasized by air brushing is sometimes helpful. This style can get real complicated and I don't recommend it for a beginner.

Right: The flames on this Chevelle feature airbrushing which creates a drop shadow effect behind the flames. This gives an illusion of depth and the flames look as if they are rising from the surface.

Below: This is a great example of 3-D flames over a granite background. The flames appear to flow out of the rock and the airbrushing drop-shadow exaggerates the depth to the flames. Design by Lil Louie.

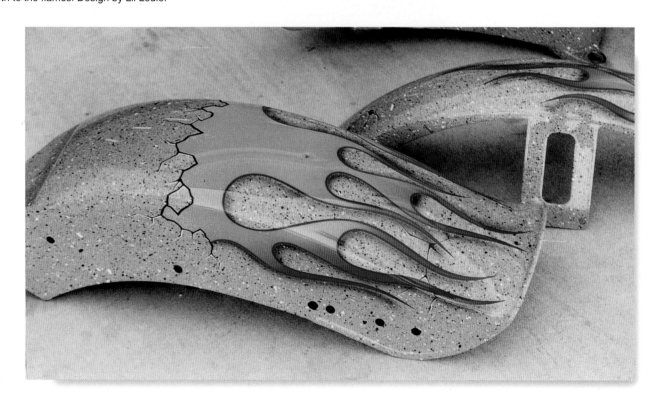

Panel Flames

Jack Giachino painted these two examples of how panel flames can be added to an existing job without getting into difficult areas such as the grill and headlights which need to be removed or masked and can involve a lot more work. Jack does it this way because so many cars have hood panels which move about and it is hard to keep the designs in alignment.

Right: The '41 Ford shows a style that doesn't involve painting the complete front of the car. Instead, the painter chose to accent the headlights and the smoothed off hood with colorful, nicely blended flames. Note how the hood patterns appear to have a scallop like effect at the front.

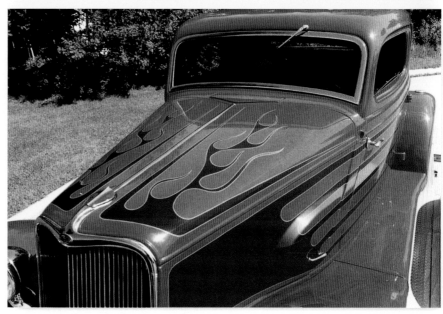

Right: The '34 Ford uses a flame pattern only on the top of the hood giving extra interest to what could have been a rather straightforward scallop paint job. The red designs compliment the orange base color and the use of the contrasting green tips and striping all combine to make the work really stand out.

Hooked End Flames

On this style the flames turn inward at the tips as they flow towards the rear of the car. Dennis Ricklefs has made this style popular on the cars he has done including these for Boyd Coddington and Pete Chapouris.

Vinyl Tape Flames

You can create different styles of pinstripe flames with the variety of vinyl tapes now on the market. This tape comes in several widths and a multitude of colors to accent any existing paint scheme. Interestingly it is still very time consuming because it needs precise application on a clean surface.

Right: This was my second chopped Mercury which I sold to Keith and Rebecca Bell. With Rebecca's help I flamed it using two sizes of vinyl striping tape. This seemingly simple design was time consuming, because to get the right look I had to do a lot of experimenting.

Sclames

I have heard this style of flame referred to as "sclames" lately by people that seem to be trying to find a new label for scallops and flames. The combination of flames and scallops is an old idea as this photo from about 1958 shows. This '57 Chevrolet shows how I feel flame designs may have progressed into scallops but I don't remember ever calling these sclames.

Right: This almost new Chevy was done by Dean Jeffries in 1957. Here we see elements of flames and scallops combined into what today some people call sclames.

Curly Tip Flames

Historically this is one of the most interesting flaming jobs of all time. Known as the "Curly Flame Ford" it was painted by Dean Jeffries in about 1953. The flame tips have a lobster claw-look which was quite different from the seaweed flames Watson was doing at the time.

Right: This photo of the famous "Curly Flamed Ford" reminds me of when I flamed my first car with similar curved flame elements.

Streamer Flames

Streamers are long, graceful waves of flames that flow along the body panels and this works well with many different body styles. Shorter bodied street rods can use this style to add an appearance of greater length. I have seen the waves effectively flowing along the fenders, across the doors and the quarter panels and even down onto the painted running boards of some cars.

Right: This '37 Ford convertible done by Lil' Louie is a good example of streamer flames. The flat side panels make for a great canvas to paint on. Note the interesting rich color scheme that compliments the de-chroming.

Louvers & Flames

Louvers are one of the most tricky and most time-consuming part of any flaming job. There are ways to make it easy by masking off the the whole row and painting them in as a solid or as a graduated color panel and by not running any tips or flickers across them. Below are a couple of examples.

Below: The hood on this Chevy truck shows how well louvers can be worked into a flame job with planning and color selection. Note how the louvers are surrounded with symmetrical fadeaway panels without any tips crossing them.

Below: Dean Jeffries flamed around the louvers on his '47 Mercury convertible simply by making all of the louvers into a solid panel and running the flame tips off the edge of panel. He did, however, insert a couple of flickers over the louvers.

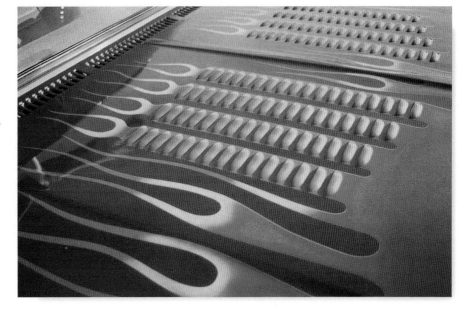

Ghost Flames

These are done in very light transparent coats of color or pearl that allow the base to show through so the appearance changes with different lighting. Normally, the flame is not striped and care must be taken to keep a clean tape edge. It is best to clear coat the complete car after the flames are unmasked to give it additional depth. This is a very subtle style of flame painting and appeals to many people because, from a distance, the flames are hard to see and the car looks like it is one color. Striping done in a color or shade almost the same as the flames gives a nice effect with this style. Airbrush highlights can also be applied under the clear coats to give more depth, especially if you add some candy toner to the first few coats.

Right: Mark Duliba painted this Chevy pickup using candy basecoats with gold pearl and tangerine toners. The flames combined with the pearl have a nice ghost effect. Multiple clear coats mixed with some mini-flake give a lot of depth.

Left: "Krazy Keith" has some really different ways of doing flames. Starting with a black pearl base, he first lightly airbrushed in the flames and smoke effects. Next, he followe with a second, heavier layer of ghost flames using more pearl. Multiple coats of transparent candy red were then applied to give a lot of depth. The colors shift with the changes in light at the viewing angles. Great work.

Flames Ideas from the Past

Above: Andy Southard shot this classic photo in Baldwin, New York, in early 1957 of a flamed '55 Chevy. It was painted black with white flames and outlined with a bright red pinstripe. Andy told me that the owners were getting ready to go for a ride and do some street racing. The Triumph in the photo shows some early striping on the tank. It was hopped up with a Chet Herbert cam and was hard to beat. Andy said he tried out Doug's bike and did his first wheelies right there in the street! The '55 Chevy is believed to be one of the first cars flamed on the East Coast. The flames are simple in design but, remember, back then there wasn't much information available other than a few magazine articles. The "fad of flames" spread quickly across the country. I like this photo a lot because it shows that flames were in style in areas other than Los Angeles.
Photo: Andy Southard

Left: This '54 Corvette was owned by Bill Acker who flamed it himself. The white car had a style all its own with the bright red flames blazing off the front fenders and hood. It was a solid color with no blends and another example of early East Coast flame work. Photo: Andy Southard.

Below: This picture was taken in Willy Wilde's Custom Shop in Gonzales, California, in 1959. The roadster's cut down doors had been done years earlier. The crude hand-painted designs on the cowl are an example of how flames may have evolved from race cars to the jalopies or hot rods of that pre-fifties' era.

Right: Small flames flickering out of the wheel opening add a tiny touch of hot rod to Willy Wilde's mildly customized '54 Corvette done in 1957.

John Hansen's '29 Hi-Boy

John was a few years older than me and I used to see a neat '40 Ford coupe parked in his driveway and an almost new '55 Ford that was black, lowered, and had real Von Dutch striping. The dash looked like it had swordfish striped on it. I remember watching Don Varner flame the coupe in shades of blue with a lot of striping.

John was building a really neat '29 Ford roadster hi-boy that he called an A-V8. Those of you who remember what an A-V8 was, know how far back his hot rodding roots went.

Soon after I opened my shop he had me put some flames on the roadster. We only flamed the sides of the hood but he brought it back later and had me do the top. This was the first hi-boy I flamed.

I was at the West Coast Kustoms event in 1996 when some people told me about a nice traditional style car that someone had just built and brought to the show. When they said it was flamed I went to find it because I am always interested in a nice flame job, especially a traditional one. I was pleasantly surprised to find John's son Jerry had brought his dad's car up for the day. It still looked just as good 25 years later.

John was always interested in what was going on in the shop and he used to come by in the roadster. Every time he had a joke to tell and he always left me with a smile. Not too long ago I was back in Salinas for a day and I saw John in the roadster ahead of me. I couldn't catch up to him but I will always remember the last time I saw him leaving a little puff of smoke off the rear tires as he took off around the corner. John passed away Dec. 7, 1996.

Below: John Hansen's '29 roadster was one of the first hot rods I flamed. He brought it to me soon after I opened shop in Salinas and I flamed the hood and side panels with traditional yellow, orange and red flames.

Below: I was very honored when Don Varner called me one day and asked if I would help him flame his Track-T. The design was created from some sketches Don had done but we worked together on the final design. I liked the combination of flames and scallops and the use of candy colors that made it stand out from most of the other street rods at the time.

Above: This is a similar Track Roadster done a few years earlier for Tom Prufer, using only flames. I am about halfway through taping inside my Salinas shop. It was painted in traditional red and yellow flames with white pinstriping by Andy Southard.

Right: With these simple, nostalgic flames this 1940 Ford sedan looks as if it may have been inspired by the cover of an October, 1956, issue of *Car Craft*.

Preparations for Flaming

I suggest that you should always start by removing all unnecessary trim such as door handles, mirrors, emblems and bumpers; this will make the job easier. Wash the car, including under the fender areas and inside the engine compartment, with a mild detergent. Do-it-yourself car washes with soap and hot water are handy if you can drive the car. Needless to-say, be sure to dry the car thoroughly and blow the water out of all the seams and jambs.

Choose a good brand of wax and grease remover and follow the instructions on the label to clean all the paint surfaces, taking great care to remove every particle of wax. Use lots of clean wiping cloths to accomplish this.

Preparation Pointers

The base coats should be completely cured before taping. After the masking is completed and you are ready to spray I suggest spraying a light coat of adhesion promoter to ensure against peeling of the designs when they are unmasked. When spraying the flame colors, the paint should be applied in medium coats. If the paint is applied too wet it may mark through the tape and have more build up along the edges. I have tried using paper to fill in some of the larger loop areas but I usually get more wrinkles which are harder to clean of dust and sanding residue.

Taping Methods

I try to apply the tape while maintaining a constant rhythm much like the same motion as when I stripe with a brush. This helps to get a roundness and flowing quality to the design. I hold the roll of 1/8-inch tape in one hand and lightly press it down as I draw the design with the tape. I try not to press it too tightly because I like to reposition the tape if the design doesn't look right. I try to lay a continous line of tape from tip to tip to get a smooth flow to the teardrop part of the design. Stopping and starting in the middle of taping can cause a glitch or a flat spot in the line.

I also pay attention to the open, unpainted areas of the work. If these areas are too small in relation to the flamed part the design might, from a distance, look like a blob of paint on the front of the car. I prefer to keep the size of the flames in harmony with each other. If there are too many different sizes or variations in the style it may tend to throw the design off balance.

Pattern Making

Once you have a satisfactory flame design on one side you can create a pattern that will enable you to duplicate the design. Take a sheet of masking paper and lay it over the flame design you have already laid out on the car, making some reference marks to the body so it will line up when it is moved to the other side.

I take a crayon or graphite pencil, lay it on its side and rub it across the surface. This will be darker where the tape is and can be seen very easily. I then take this sheet of paper and lay it on a piece of sheet rock or some other semi-hard surface and run the pounce wheel along the dark line, punching a series of small holes in the paper. I use the sheet rock because it allows the wheel to puncture through the paper easily.

After the pattern is punched out, I turn the paper over and using a piece of 180 or 220 sandpaper, I lightly sand the back side of the design to open up the holes, taking care not to tear the paper.

Using the reference marks, I position the pattern on the opposite side of the car and, after it's aligned properly, I use a pounce bag or chalk bag and rub it along the perforations. When the paper is removed the pattern will appear as a dotted line that can be used to duplicate the design with the outline tape.

Incidentally, I keep some of my old pounce patterns and use them on other cars for inspiration or just to get my ideas started. I do not use the exact same design but it seems to get the job going faster. If I use an old pattern I will modify and completely change the design before I am done to make it individual to the car I am working on. This works really well with popular body styles like late model pickups. I had to do two identically flamed Camaro race cars for a customer at one time and the creation of these patterns really speeded up the job. Also, if you keep the patterns on file they are available if the car is damaged or needs to be repainted.

Finish Taping

Once I have a final outline on the complete car, I am ready to start covering the areas that are not going to be painted. I like to use 2-inch tape for this because it collects less dirt and gives a smoother surface that is easier to clean. I apply a piece of 2-inch tape over the 1/8-inch outline and press it down tightly. I keep the tape as straight and flat as possible doing a small area at a time. If you try to follow the outline tape with the wide tape it causes more wrinkles and possible leaks. A poorly masked surface may hold bits of dirt that can get in the paint and it is usually harder to unmask if there is no method to the masking process. The underlying tape design will show through slightly. Lightly rubbing a piece of crayon across it helps to make it easier to see.

Door Jamb Masking

If you are not flaming the jambs I recommend masking around the edge of the opening and sealing off any areas you do not want painted. There is a special tape made for masking jambs which looks like a rope, is easy to use and saves some time. Check for it at your local paint store.

If you want designs inside these areas, mask them before filling in the outer areas. Then mask everything so you can open the doors and the hood as you are spraying. You will find that this is a lot more work and on most cars it isn't worth the extra effort.

Final Design

After the car is completely masked, stand back again and look at how you are doing with the design. I like to compare it to a photographic negative at this point. Everything masked will be the color of the car. The unmasked areas will be the flames. At this stage you can still pull back if you are beginning to have doubts, the surface of the car has not been sanded or painted yet. This is the point of no return.

Painting Preparation

Time to sand the shiny areas: Using 3M gray scuff pads very carefully, dull the exposed paint, trying not to damage the tape edges. After this is done, blow the loose dust and dirt off the surface and clean it again with wax and grease remover and clean wipes. Repair any torn or damaged places and clean it again. If you have touched the surface with bare fingers, the oils in your skin may cause problems in the paint. Clean your painting area walls and floor. After parking the car I like to tape the paper to the floor to keep overspray from getting under the paper. Make sure you have a clean surface treated with wax and grease remover and lots of clean, wiping rags on hand.

At this point any damaged edges should be repaired and holes in the masking tape should be found. The floor should be dampened but don't make puddles or splash the car—a garden sprayer works well. Wipe with Tac Rag. Include all the covered areas as well as the area to be painted. Sometimes there is dust on the paper that will blow into the paint. Have all your materials ready for mixing. A clean table, covered with 36-inch paper, works just fine.

Basic Paint Requirements

Many of the new paint systems need catalysts and reducers for each of the different coats so check with your supplier and make sure you have on hand the necessary materials to get the job done. Be sure to read and understand the instructions on the label. Many of the paint manufacturers are not putting instruction labels on paint cans any more because the paint is supposed to be for professional use only. Paint suppliers should have tech sheets for all the paint they sell. If you are not a trained professional and are doing the work at home, or in a hobby shop, you may have trouble even buying the paint in some areas. You should also be aware of hazardous waste disposal procedures.

Painting

When I paint, I have a graceful motion. If I am by myself, in a good mood, with some of the right music going I have been known to dance around the car while painting! I enjoy doing my flames.

I do my painting in a shop that has the proper equipment and sometimes I have a trusted painter apply the base coats and clears for me. The paint industry is changing so rapidly it would be useless to go into exact brands and materials in this book. What is working for me today may be obsolete or unavailable in your area or mine in the near future. The ideal shop for flaming is a well lit, high tech, roomy booth with a few helpers to keep things clean and get you what you need when you need it.

Spray Guns

Although my first spray gun was an airbrush, I soon found it didn't hold enough material to do what I needed. I use my full size DeVilbiss spray gun much like an airbrush and I feel it is the same thing although some artists don't seem to think so. Learning to use the spray gun is important and it can't be done just by adjusting the equipment and pulling the trigger. If you are going to do this artistically it doesn't help if you have to fight the equipment. Don't expect perfection the first time. Doing something every day also helps to make things go smoother when the job is important.

Equipment for Flaming

Above: This is a selection of some of the tools I use for my flame work. Items shown include rulers, spray guns, fresh-air breathing system, air-brush, pounce box, tape, hand cleaners, camera, pinstripe brushes, transfer paper, gloves and sketch pad.

For many jobs I've filled the back of my pickup with equipment and materials necessary to do a complete job, and sometimes I've flamed a car in someone else's well-equipped shop, armed with only a piece of chalk and a couple of rolls of 1/8-inch tape.

Most of the equipment I show here is what I use to create my designs and prepare for spraying the paint. Because of the diversity of paint spraying equipment I only briefly describe it. If you're not familiar with automotive spray painting, I recommend finding someone who can show you what is involved, or have them do that part of the job for you. With the advanced technology that is so essential to quality work these days, it would be impossible to try to teach anyone how to use this rapidly changing equipment in just a few paragraphs. Personally, I didn't have much success with my

work until I took the time to learn how to use the equipment and materials properly.

Stabilo Pencils

These pencils are designed to be used on paper, glass, plastic and metal. They are water soluble and the marks can be removed with a damp rag. If the entire car is being clear coated it is a good idea to scrub the surface with a medium scuff pad and Ajax cleanser, or one of the new sanding compounds such as Final-Sand. This is to ensure that all of the pencil marks are removed before the clear coats are applied.

Chalk

I use chalk if I am sketching on the surface of the car. Chalk is easier to wipe off. I do not recommend using felt markers, ball-point pens or crayons.

Pounce Box

This is a hand-held box with a soft cloth bag attached to the top which is filled with a powdered chalk similar to the blue chalk used by the construction industry for their chalk lines. The box is refillable through an opening in the top that is fitted with a plug. There are different colors of chalk available but I usually like to use blue. After the pattern is fitted to the surface of the car the pounce box is lightly patted and/or rubbed along the perforations in the paper. When the paper is removed there should a fine dotted line outlining the flame design. Gently blow away the excess powder (don't wipe!). You should now be able to follow the outline with the outline tape and duplicate the pattern from the other side. Pounce boxes are available at sign supply stores and some craft stores. The chalk is available at a builder's supply store. If you can't find a box or chalk, an old sock filled with talcum powder will get the job done!

Pounce Wheel

For many years I used an elaborate system of tracing a pattern onto the paper, then cutting it out with scissors or a razor blade. Next, I would tape it to the car and measure all the tips and loops, then trace around it with a Stabilo pencil. It was a lot of work. A few years ago I took a sign painting class from Mr. J of New Jersey who showed me how to use a pounce wheel. I'd had the wheel in my tool box for many years and I'd seen my mother using one for dress patterns but had never thought it would save me time. Pounce wheels are used to make a pattern in the paper by punching a series of holes along a drawn or traced design. By rubbing chalk powder through the holes in the paper pattern the image is transferred to the surface of the vehicle. The back side of the paper must then be lightly sanded to take the burrs off the holes. Pounce wheels can be found at craft stores, fabric shops and sign supply warehouses.

Electro-Pounce

The electric pounce burns small holes through the paper. It produces the same type of pattern as the pounce wheel and the back side of the paper does not have to be sanded to open the holes. A steel backing is necessary to burn the pattern and magnets may be used to hold the paper in place. It's a lot easier to make smaller and more intricate patterns with an electric pounce, however, you should be very careful while using this tool as it produces an electric shock if you don't wear protective gloves. I have zapped myself more than once and it was usually because I was in too much of a hurry to put on the gloves.

Masking Tape

There is no substitute for quality masking tape—do not make the mistake of going to a cheaper grade of tape just to save a few dollars. I've tried many different brands and 3M tape has always worked best for me.

Outline Tape

For most of my outlining I like to use regular 3M crepe masking tape in the 1/8-inch and 1/4-inch sizes. This size and type of tape is easy to reposition. I try to keep a slight amount of tension as the line is being applied to the surface, and have found that the regular masking tape doesn't stretch or go out of shape like so many other vinyl tapes.

Fill-in Tape

I use 1/2-inch and 2-inch widths of 3M masking tape when I am filling the open areas of the flame patterns. If applied smoothly it will give the best seal against paint bleeding through and the surface will be easier to keep clean of overspray dust.

Vinyl Tape

Vinyl tape stretches out of shape if it is pulled too tight and it is also more difficult to get it to flow around corners without wrinkling. I find the vinyl tape leaves marks in the basecoat surface if it hasn't cured properly. It works well for long straight lines that are not going to be outlined with a pinstripe. The vinyl comes in a variety of smaller widths that are very good for small intricate designs but I personally find it harder to work with on larger areas.

Razor Blades

Buy a box of single edge razor blades. These are inexpensive so use as many as you need because they will get dull quickly.

X-Acto Knives

These have a sharp point that is more maneuverable in intricate areas. The point makes it easier to cut through the tape but be careful not to cut into the painted surface as it is very difficult to repair. The point dulls quickly so I like to have a small piece of fine sandpaper or a sharpening stone handy to keep my blade sharp. If the blade dull the tape may tear and give you a ragged edge.

Spray Guns

High Volume Low Pressure (HVLP) spray guns are required in many areas now. Be sure you have enough air volume to operate it as it requires a steady flow of air at the gun to atomize the paint properly. This is a major problem if you are trying to paint at home with a small compressor. I used DeVilbiss JGA guns for most of my work and I even have a couple set up with two quart

pressure pots. These I use for spraying on clear coats when we cleared the entire car to eliminate the edge patterns. I have used a touch-up gun to blend the colors around the edges and on the tips but, most of the time I use my full-size gun, I can shut it down to a small pattern and feather the trigger better than with the others. Some painters use an airbrush but unless you are working very detailed stuff such as highlights, murals, and tiny designs, this is not needed.

Airbrush

When I started trying to be a custom painter my first paint gun was an airbrush. After seeing Roth and Jeffries at car shows airbrushing shirts I thought cars and shirts could be painted with the same equipment. I soon found out an airbrush didn't hold enough paint to spray cars. They are great for small objects and motorcycles and do use less material. I have found them fragile and it's a good idea to have more than one of them around in case it gets clogged up. I always have several and keep them in good working order.

Transferite ®

There is new a product called "Transferite" which is a backing material for vinyl lettering. This paper was not meant to be a masking paper and has its limitations. Some of its problems are that it doesn't adhere as well and sometimes it lifts, causing paint leaks. The paint seems to build up on the paper and cause fuzz and lint. It is thin and doesn't seem as resistant to strong paints and it can't be left on too long. I use it like an artist's frisket paper for small areas and airbrushing.

Masking Paper

Use a good quality masking paper for covering the larger areas. This paper is sold in a variety of sizes. Plastic sheeting is also available to "bag" the car. This is essential for protecting the rest of the car when using the new two-stage paints.

Striping Brushes

When I started striping in the mid-fifties there was only one type of brush available—the Mack Touch-Up brush sold in auto parts stores. I would trim and cut them, trying to make them do what I wanted. When one was broken in I would then use it until it was worn out. Today there are many different brushes available. For striping the edges on my flames I use an Excaliber brush that has been developed by Mr. J. These brushes are shorter in length and I find them easier to use on curves and tight corners. I no longer have to trim and break in my brushes. If you have trouble finding brushes in your area ask the local sign painter where he gets his supplies.

Safety Equipment

Safety measures were not thought about back in the early years. The only protective equipment I used was a paper surgical mask. I can remember spitting up metalflake for days after painting my '51 Merc'.

Important: Check with your local paint shop, and county health department about the latest respirators and clean- air systems. Don't attempt any work without the right safety equipment.

Equipment List

Stabilo, Pentel and crayon pencils
Chalk,
Ruler, yardstick, tape measure
Tape, variety of sizes at least 1/8, 1/4, 3/4, 1 .1/2-inch
Vinyl tape
Pounce wheel, chalk box, chalk
Masking paper at least 12-inch or 18-inch
Plastic car cover for masking
Sand paper and scuff pads
Wax and grease remover
Paper towels for clean up of spills
Quality wipes for cleaning car
Containers for mixing paint
Stir sticks
Strainers for paint
Notebook or sketch pad, pen or pencil
X-Acto type knife,
Razor blades
A section of sheet rock to use the pounce wheel on
Steel sheet for electro pounce pattern
Striping supplies
Brushes: Xcalibar, Mack, etc.
One shot enamel, reducer
H.O.K. striping urethane, reducer, catalyst
Mixing cups ,paper or plastic
Popsicle sticks
Palette or old magazines
Hand protection creme, hand cleaner
Apron.

Camera

I like to photograph my work so I can see my progress through the years and self-critique my work. It gives me something I can show to my clients.

Tom Akeman and I talked about flaming his '32 hi boy roadster for about a year before it actually happened. One minor difficulty was the fact that he lived on the Marshall Islands in the South Pacific! We talked back and forth on the phone about the rod and subsequently he had it delivered to my place from San Jose where he was keeping it at a friend's house.

He wanted the work to be finished in time to drive it to the Father's Day Roadster Show in Los Angeles. We had about five weeks to do it and he left the design up to me. He wanted flames on the sides and their color to match the interior. I laid out the flames at my studio and then the paint job was done at the Espinosa Body Shop in Santa Rosa, California.

The roadster had been built a few years previously and was a nice example of "a hi-tech street rod." There was nothing wrong with the way the car looked but Tom wanted to update it and do something different.

He asked me to do the flame job on his roadster as I had flamed cars and motorcycles for his friends R.H.Jones, Tom Prufer, and Nick Ellis.

Left: First, I washed the car using a mild detergent and thoroughly dried it. Usually, I remove any parts that interfere with the work but this one was so smoothed off there was nothing to remove.

Right: I "draw" on the surface with 1/8-inch tape to get some design ideas. I take my time doing this part of the job; the layout is very important. I don't use a pencil or chalk much at first but sometimes they help get me started. I did this design after playing around with one that was too busy.

Left: I made a tracing of the final design using a piece of lightweight masking paper loosely taped over the area I wanted to copy. By rubbing across the paper with the side of a black crayon the tape pattern starts to appear.

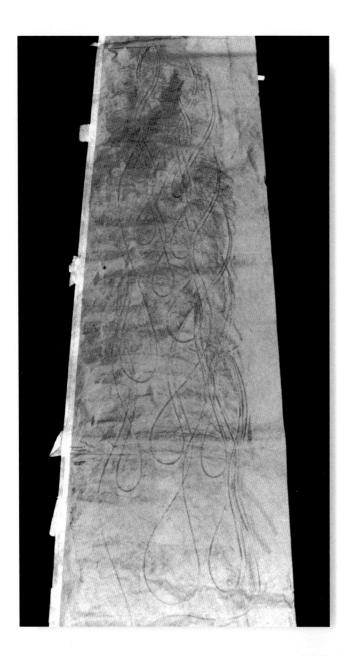

Left: This is the masking paper pattern. Here, you can see the reference marks at the door gap lines. I also cut notches at the door gaps or sometimes holes where the locks or hinges are located. This makes it easy to line up the pattern. Since the pattern will be reversed on the opposite side, the crayon marks will not be visible.

Right: These are the tools I used to make my pounce pattern. Two different sizes of pounce wheels are shown. The smaller one is used for tighter corners. You can see the holes in the paper if you look closely. After you use a wheel, lightly sand the back side of the pattern with 220 sandpaper. This will open the perforations for a more distinct pattern. The pounce box holds a refillable chalk pad. As you can see, it is well worn and ready to be changed. When the pad wasn't available, sometimes I have used an old sock filled with powdered chalk or talcum powder.

Left: Now that I have a final pattern I remove all my tape designs which I had applied only as reference designs. The surface must be thoroughly cleaned with a good grade of wax and grease remover. Positioning the pattern on the car, I use my reference marks for alignment. Then I lightly rub the pad along the design, dusting the chalk through the holes in the pattern. This leaves an outline on the car which I use as a taping guide.

Right: The chalk pattern should look like this. You can now carefully blow away the excess chalk. This leaves a clear dotted outline for final taping.

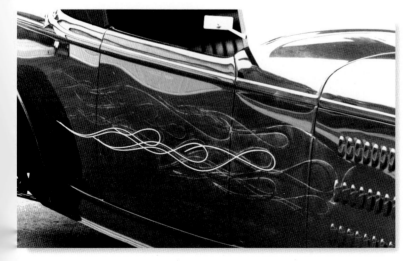

Left: As you can see, I am not following the design exactly at this point because as I work I may decide to change it. The design is not fixed in my mind yet.

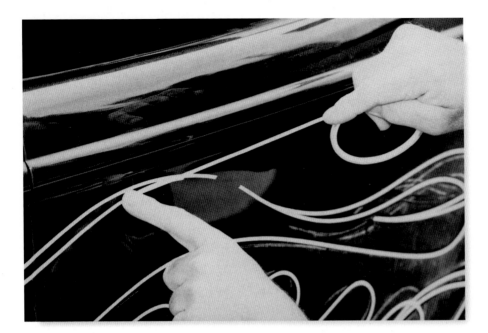

Left: I lightly press the 1/8-inch tape so it can be repositioned if it is uneven or doesn't flow right. If the tape is pressed too hard or pulled too tight it will tear or stretch, making a more awkward line.

Right: I "draw" with the tape, pressing lightly with my finger almost like I'm pointing to where I want it to go. Here I am doing what I call a "lick" or a "flicker" to extend the design. I like to make these appear to be an extension of one of the flame ends. It is a good way to extend the design a little further without making it appear to be too heavy.

Right: This is how the taping should look although the design is not the final one I used.

Below: After the outline is done I use 2-inch or 1.1/2-inch tape and cover over areas of the surface that I don't want to paint. I have found that the 1.1/2-inch tape is considerably cheaper than 2-inch.

Left: I apply one strip at a time and cut the excess away by running the razor blade along the 1/8-inch line, being very careful to cut only the 2-inch tape and not go through the second layer into the paint. I use a lot of single-edge razor blades. They dull fast but I can control them easier. I use X-Acto knives because I can hold them like a striping brush and sometimes it is faster but I have found that X-Acto knives can cut too deeply if you are not careful. I keep a piece of 1000-grit sandpaper handy and sharpen the blade often for a cleaner cut. The blades are not too expensive but changing them takes some time.

Right: After everything is covered, I cut the tape at all the openings so the side panels can be removed and the doors opened.

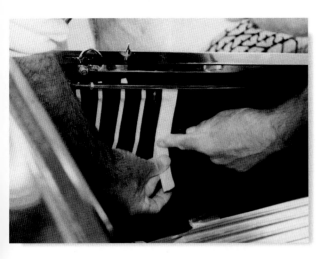

Left: On louvered cars the paint makes a mess if you don't correctly mask off the openings. First, mask off the inside edge of the louver with narrow tape then run your wider tape across lengthwise to completely seal off against overspray.

Below: You can see how all the louvers don't have to be covered but the inside surface of the ones to be painted must be protected with tape.

Left: I then covered the masked openings with 2" to protect the motor from overspray and wrapped the complete motor with paper and plastic. It is important to make sure the fire wall is protected also. It is a lot of work but much easier than cleaning up overspray.

Left: When the masking is finished, the louvers should look like this. They are open but the overspray can't get through.

Below: Where the flames cross over you can see that the 1/8-inch tape will have to be removed before the base is sprayed. I sometimes make a sketch at this point so I will know how many crossovers there are. When the base is painted you will have a hard time seeing where to re-mask to get the crossover effect.

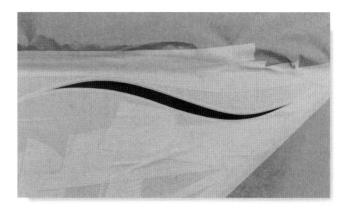

Below: Sometimes a detail like this flicker can make a design more interesting and also add length to the flames in an awkward area.

Above: Before the crossover tape has been removed you may want to make a rubbing stencil to use as a reference when the tips have to be remasked.

Below: After the crossover tape has been removed it should look like this.

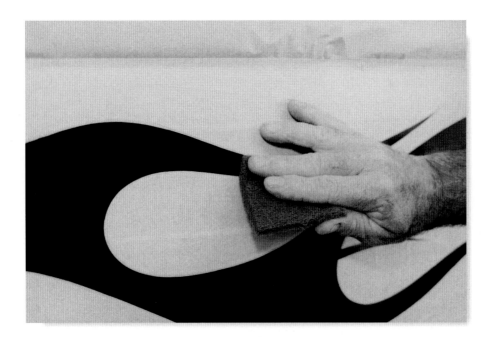

Left: Here I am using a 3M grey scuff pad to dull the exposed surface, being careful not to damage the taped edge.

Below: The scuffing residue must be blown away with compressed air and the surface should be given a final clean with wax and grease remover. It is a good idea to wear protective gloves because the solvents in the wax and grease remover can be absorbed through the skin into the blood stream.

Above: I then tape off the whole car with plastic sheeting and use wider tape to seal it to the floor. This prevents overspray entering under the car. The new two-part paint systems are very adhesive and when they get under the paper they stick to everything if you don't tape the car off completely.

Below: I then wet the floor lightly making sure there are no puddles. A garden sprayer works well for this and can be kept in the booth to re-wet the floor during spraying.

Left: I blow the car off again with compressed air and use a clean tac rag to remove all dust and lint. Be sure to wipe the complete surface including the tape and paper before painting.

Below: On this job, I sprayed a clear adhesion promoter as a sealer before any colors were applied.

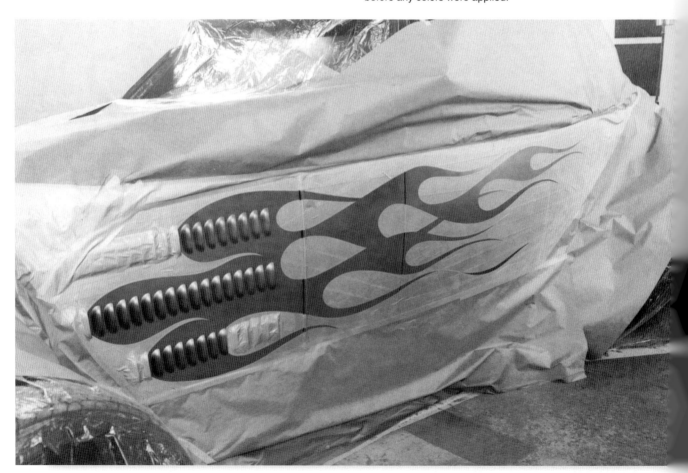

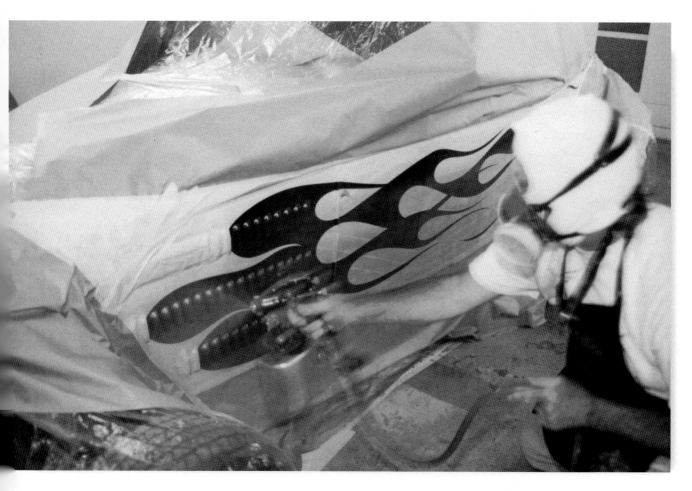

Above: I used light grey metallic for a base and tinted it with a little burgundy Koncentrate. The paint density was enough to allow me to lay the color down in three medium coats.

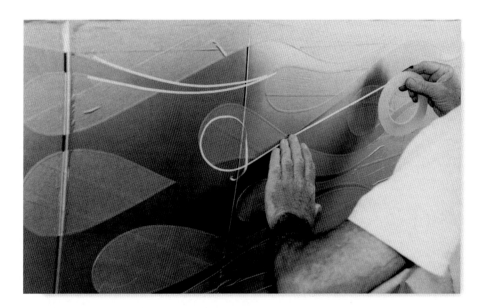

Above: After the base had dried, I began taping the cross-over areas. I try to do this next step as quickly as possible. If the tape is left on too long, it will mark the surface.

Below: To define the cross-overs, I make shields from 2-inch tape and turn the air pressure and pattern down on my paint gun. Note how I turn up the tape to form a valley. This gives me protection from most overspray when I shoot the tip.

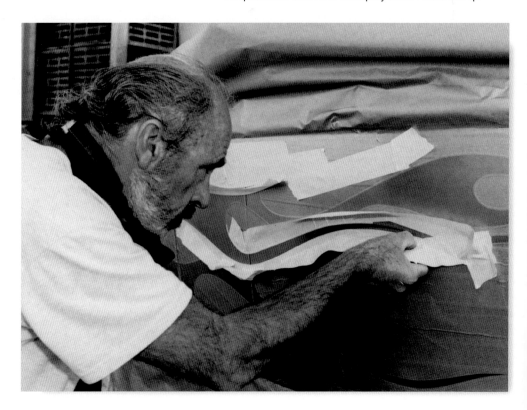

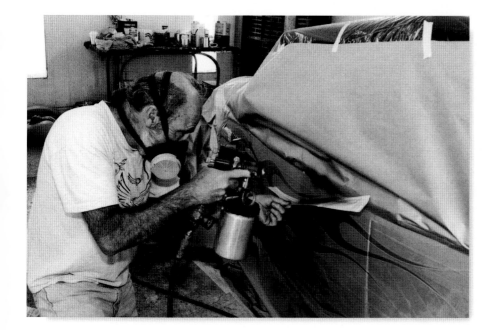

Left: A smaller gun may work better for some of this work but I prefer to use my full-size guns as I usually find it gives me a better blend. If I'm not sure about overspray, I use more paper for protection.

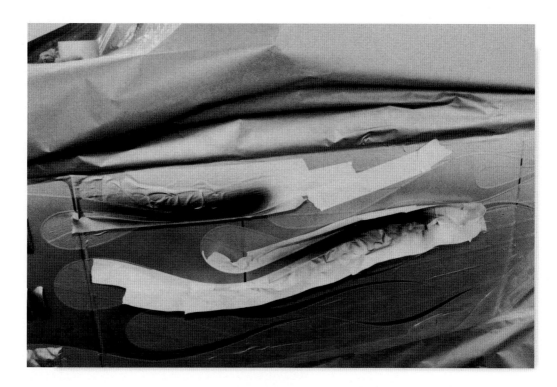

Above: The blends should look like this. They may seem to be too dark but this will change when it is unmasked. I sometimes carefully pull back some of the tape to see how the contrast of the colors is going to look. Be sure to re-mask completely if you do this.

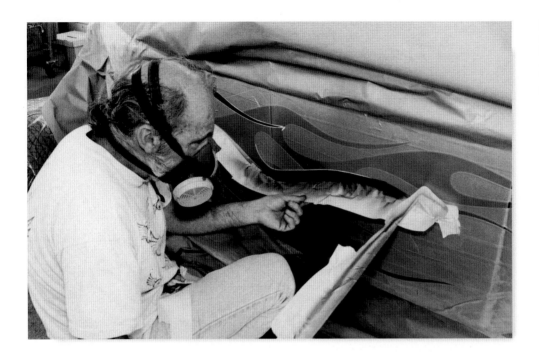

Left: After the paint has dried sufficiently, I begin unmasking. I like to remove everything but the outline tape, leaving it for last. This way I am not fighting a mass of tape and paper.

Below: Get the big stuff out of the way then all you have to worry about is the small outline tape. Note how I am pulling back on the 1/8-inch tape to "cut" the edge of the paint cleanly.

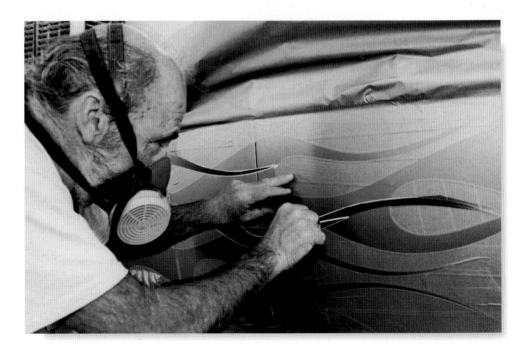

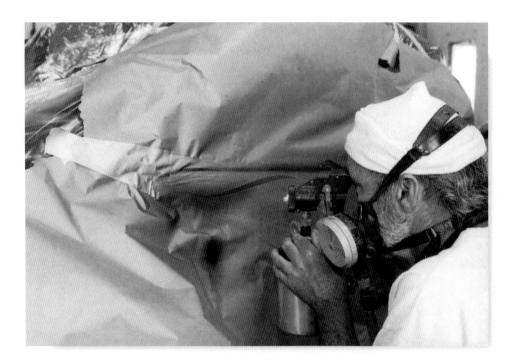

Above: Next, I spray the rest of the tips the same color. I try not to miss any because they are hard to see after the base coat is sprayed. It is extremely important that I count my paint gun passes to get the colors the same. Sometimes I make guide marks every few inches with a pencil on the tape to indicate where to start the blend.

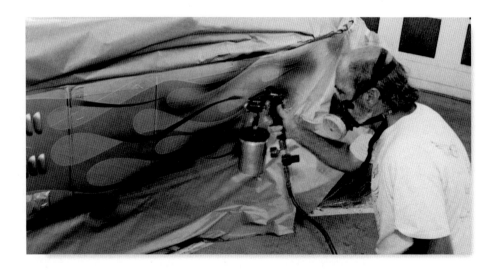

Above: After the tips are darkened I blend along the edges with a more transparent version of the same color. This final color softens the effect. It is a good idea to spray a few coats of clear to protect the blended areas just in case the surface needs to be sanded.

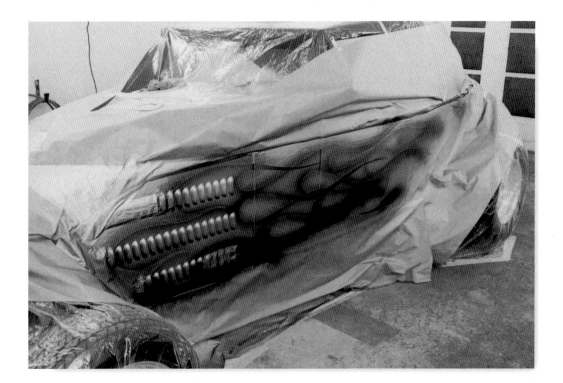

Left: The final coats are urethane clear and they make the color stand out. Even these black and white pictures show the difference.

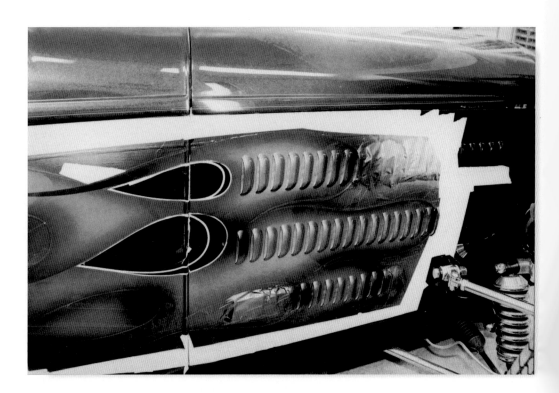

Above: At last it can be unmasked. Simply remove all of the taping in the reverse order. Plastic and paper first, working your way down to the 1/8-inch outline tape. A razor blade is handy for trimming difficult areas.

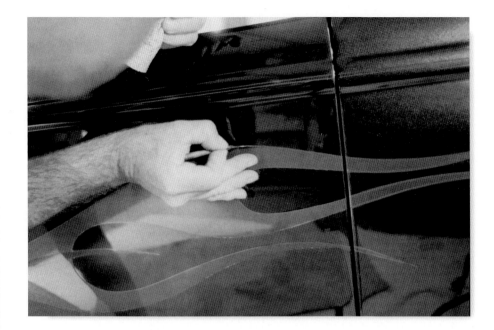

Left: Next, I lightly sand and polish the flame edges, then clean the car again thoroughly before striping. The edges were striped in a color that matched the interior, using One Shot striping enamel.

Below: After the striping was finished, I let it dry overnight and cleaned it up with a light glaze to remove any smudges.

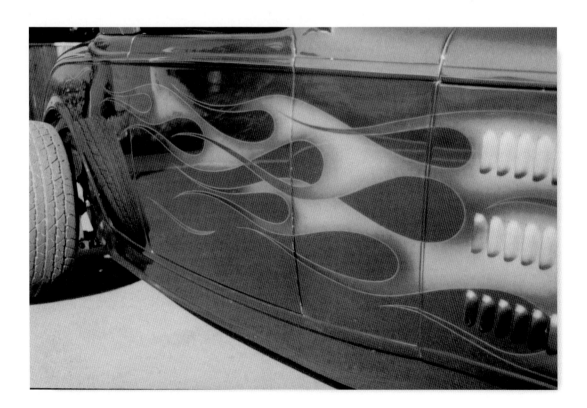

"Ghost Flaming a Pickup"

This 1995 Chevrolet truck I did with Mark Duliba in Salinas, California, for Reuben Cazarez. Mark was my main painter in Salinas for many years so we had done a lot of nice work together and this truck is one of the latest.

I did all of the designs and taping. The color scheme and the double ghost flame ideas were Mark's. He gave me an idea of what he wanted and I set about layering on the tape.

I did the taping over several weeks because it is a fairly complex design. Once I had all the tape design done, Mark took the Chevy into the paint shop and shot on the spectacular coat of pearl orange with ghost flames.

Above: Mark had the truck based with a pearl orange, and color-sanded, ready for me to start my layouts. I did more than one design to get what I was looking for. On this job I made two different patterns because of the double flame idea.

Above: Here, I am making my pounce pattern by rubbing the flat side of a crayon across 36-inch paper to show the 1/8-inch tape pattern. I also make reference marks at door openings, door handles and body lines to help align the paper when I re-apply it later.

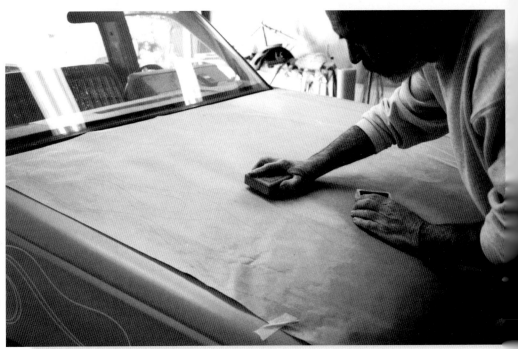

Right: After using a pounce wheel to make a series of holes in the paper, I align the pattern on the truck and use my pounce box to rub chalk through the holes in the pattern.

Left: Here you can see the chalk lines after the paper is removed. I then lightly blow away the excess chalk.

Above: I follow the dots with 1/8-inch tape for the final design. Some painters use a fine line vinyl tape to get a cleaner edge when they get to this point. I like to use regular crepe masking tape because it is more maneuverable and can be re-positioned easily.

Left: Here, the body is covered with 2-inch tape. Note how the hood gap is cut so that it can be opened. I also do the same with the doors so that the truck can be moved. Check carefully for missed areas where the paint can bleed through as this is very hard to correct when doing ghost flames.

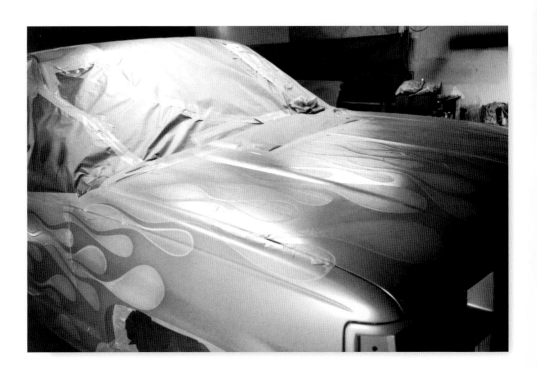

Above: We begin spraying the flames using clear mixed with a light blend of candy orange toner. Next, adding more toner, you blend along the edges to give it the fade-away effect.

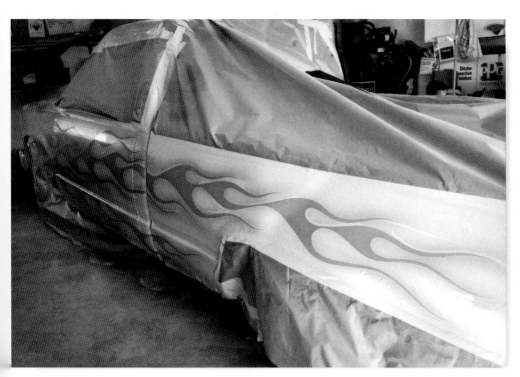

Left: This shows the first set of flames already sprayed. You can see that the 2-inch tape provides a clean surface so the overspray and dust can be removed easily with the tac rag. Note how the paint has been lightly misted on. Because of the transparent nature of the tinted clear, the pearl basecoats show through giving the ghost flame effect.

Above: Here, Mark is removing the 1/8-inch tape. Note how he is pulling the tape back on itself to cut a cleaner edge. After unmasking the truck, Mark completely color sanded and cleared the truck in preparation for the second set of flames.

Left: This shows the first set of flames already sprayed and the second set 1/8-inch tape layout in progress. After the first flames were sprayed the truck was clear coated and color sanded to keep the edge of the designs from showing.

Above: Another shot of the second layout. The areas that show two tape lines are where I am changing the design to make it flow better. I will only paint to the inside tape edge.

Above: This shot shows the flames on the roof. We wanted them on the roof but we didn't want to go clear across the top because it's a lot more work, so we just did the outer edges.

Above: To start the design on the tailgate I applied vertical and diagonal tape lines to find the center. Using these lines gives me a guide for the area I want to cover and helps me keep the design in proportion. I taped this design on the left side trying to achieve a fireball effect from the center of the panel. Next, I made a crayon pattern, then removed all the tape. With this half of the design I made my pounce pattern by doubling the paper on the vertical center line and burned through both layers with the Electro-Pounce pattern maker. This way, I have one sheet of paper with a symmetri cal pattern for the whole tailgate. Although I liked the flames on the rolled pan, we decided against including them in the final design.

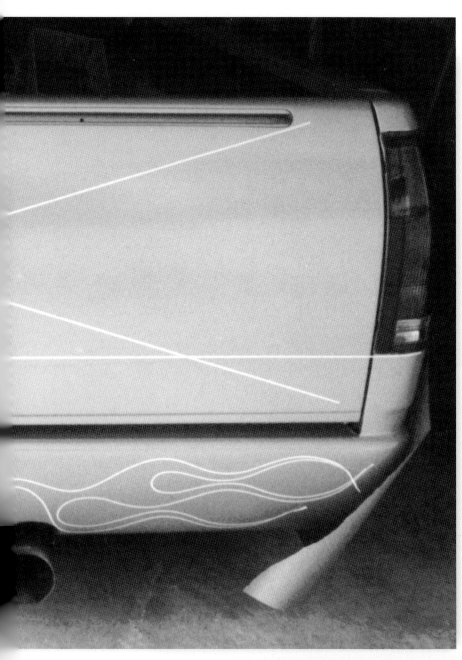

Below: This is the tailgate masked up and ready to paint. The small piece is a panel Mark used to test his colors. This is a very good idea especially with the ghost flames.

John Schipp's '32 Ford Tudor Sedan "Hell Rod" really lived up to its name! John and I had spoken about flaming the Tudor a year before I got to do the job, I thought it would be fun to flame this car in primer or a flat finish so he could show it off for the summer. However, when John decided he wanted high quality paint instead of primer, the '32 turned out to be "a hell of a job" but I got it done with lots of help. This wild, outrageously flamed, black rod came out just right and everyone loved it. Hell Rod has since appeared in numerous magazines.

Below: The body is in black basecoat and has been sanded and I have started to lay out designs. I like to draw with the tape and use regular 1/8-inch masking tape for this because I can pull it back up and reapply it without stretching it out of shape. By drawing with the tape instead of chalk I can visualize the design better. I like to stand back and look at my work and I find that chalk marks are too hard to see from a distance. Trying to follow a chalk or pencil line too closely can make it crooked or jerky.

Above: The grille was so short I had trouble coming up with a design for it. A car with no hood and a skinny grille presents a design problem because you have very little space on which to wo up the design. John, the owner wanted to try it without any flames and eventually that's how we did it.

Below: This is another idea we didn't use. The firewall was so big and flat I thought I would try some designs there also. The cowl area was so short, the flames appeared too stubby, so I tried to make them look like they were coming from behind the motor and up onto the cowl. This design idea can be done on something like a late-model truck with a lot of surface but on a small and complicated car like this, it is a different situation. I began thinking about how the motor was a big part of the overall look of this car and that designs in the firewall area might be too much.

Left: Once I had got the design set as I wanted it, I started filling in with 2-inch masking tape.

Below: After I applied the 2-inch tape, I used a single-sided razor blade to trim off the excess tape that covered the area to be painted. I press very gently on the blade so I don't cut through the lower layers or into the body surface.

Left: The flames on the roof were done to cover up imperfections. It is fairly common to use the design to cover or disguise imperfections in the base paint. Unfortunately this puts pressure on the designer and can limit the artistic part of the job. Here I am almost finished but I still need to add a few more licks to the roof.

Below: The taping is all done on the rear. It was my favorite part of the job as it even looks good just in tape.

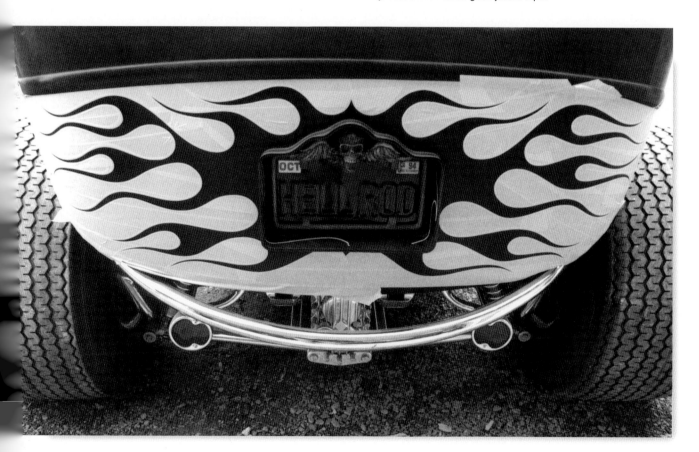

Left: These were the two basic colors that Dennis Hartwig of Creative Concepts in Sebastopol, California, mixed for Hell Rod first base colors. The third color he mixed later.

Below: Dennis painted the car in light grey sealer first. Here, he is cleaning the car with a tac-rag before applying the first layer of color. On a dark colored car, I recommend starting with a coat of white which helps the more transparent yellow cover with less coats of paint.

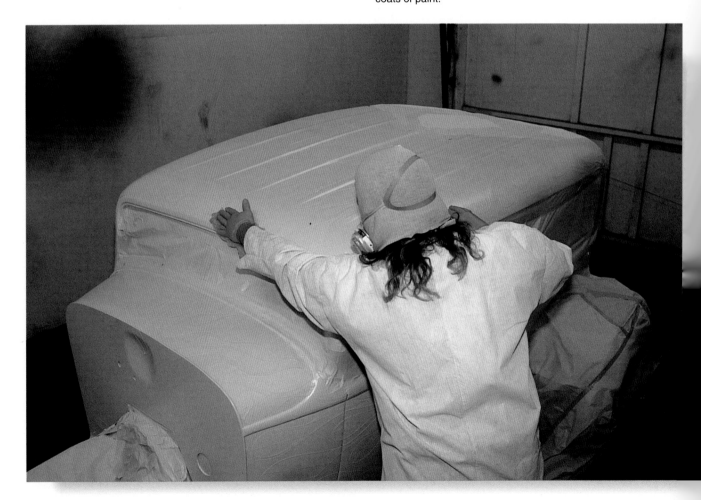

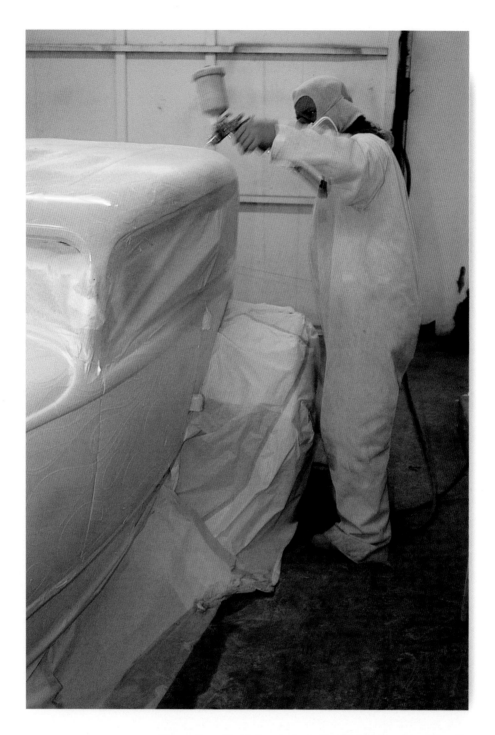

Above: Here, Dennis is spraying color. These colors are solid and the pictures show how hard it is to see the flames after they are sprayed. I make sure that all the tips are done the same way. If one is missed it's very noticeable, but it can be touched up later. Sometimes I make Stabilo pencil marks to show how far to blend but I have found I need to be careful when wiping the car with wax and grease remover so that these marks are not smudged into the flame colors.

Above: The first layer of yellow is going on all over the flame surfaces. Dennis is seen here rigged out in his charcoal filter face mask and full coveralls.

Above: The second color is being sprayed here. It is applied across the center of the flames and once again Dennis starts on the roof of the car and works his way down and around. Because of the complexity of the flames on this car, he had to remember to get all the flickers and chassis rail flames.

Above: Note the closeness of the gun to the car and how little paint Dennis is applying. Knowing how to accurately trigger the flow of paint from the gun to the surface is critical and requires much practice. This stage of the painting determines the width of the blend into the next color.

Above: Dennis has now finished with the second color. Note how little orange is actually on the car and how it blends out around the license plate in a fan. Also note how well the car is masked off to prevent overspray. Before he applied the clear coat he sealed the car to the ground.

Above: The rear view of Hell Rod shows the painting completed. Note how the tips are spotted in and the center area shows only a little yellow. See the opening page to this chapter for a finished view of the same section.

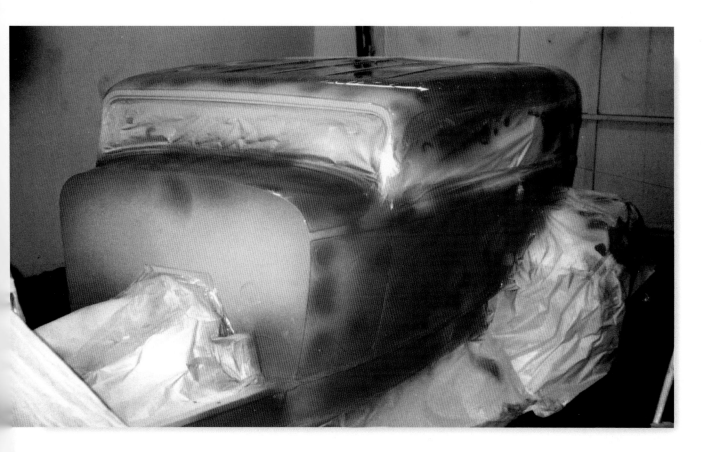

Above: This front view of the finished painting shows the car looking like a spotted leopard. A point to remember—the more complex the design, the more complex the painting and the harder it is to remember to get every flicker and tip.

Right: The taped edges sometimes come out ragged when the tape is removed. It is relatively easy to clean when the job is finished but it still had to have a pinstripe to finish it off. This was not a problem as the style of flame I wanted had to have a striped edge. The car was striped in blue with a fat line that finished it off nicely.

Motorcyle flames

Motorcycles have always been part of my business. Looking back it seems that bikers and lowriders trusted me to use my imagination a lot more than the street rodders and custom owners.

Many times that made the work more gratifying and, because bikes have been a large part of my work I decided to include a motorcycle how-to-do-it in the book. There are many great painters doing motorcycles today and it is impossible to show even a fraction of the superb styles and designs that are being done.

In this section I will show how I do a double flame design on a tank and fender set. I hope this will spark your imagination and show some techniques and styles that may enhance and make your work easier.

Above: To begin the paint on this Harley-Davidson I had all the parts stripped by media blasting at Christensen Coatings. This leaves a smooth surface and must be sanded before priming. In the photo the tank is still in bare metal but the fenders are already painted and sanded again for the first set of flames.

Left: The parts were prepped and primed using the correct procedures for the material I was using. I then sprayed a black basecoat, followed with a light coat of pearl. This made the parts appear to be charcoal metallic but a few coats of candy violet toner mixed with clear, made the paint look black from some angles with a strong purple or burgundy highlight.

Right: After the basecoats were cured and sanded I taped the first set of flames using 1/8-inch masking tape. Since there were going to be two sets of flames, I tried to leave enough open area for the second set of designs.

94

Above: After I have a design I am satisfied with, on one of the tanks I make my pounce pattern. Positioning a piece of masking paper on the surface, I make some reference or alignment marks so I can reposition it on the other half of the tank. Next, I make the pattern by rubbing across the surface of the paper with the side of a crayon. The raised tape on the tank forms a ridge which leaves darker lines on the paper where the crayon strikes it through the paper. I then use this rubbing for my pattern.

Right: Using an Electro Pounce, I place the paper on a sheet of steel and very carefully trace the crayon pattern, burning a series of perforations in the paper. Because of the high voltage, it is a good idea to wear gloves when using an electric pounce. As you can see in the photo, I am not doing so and shortly after this photo was taken I got zapped.

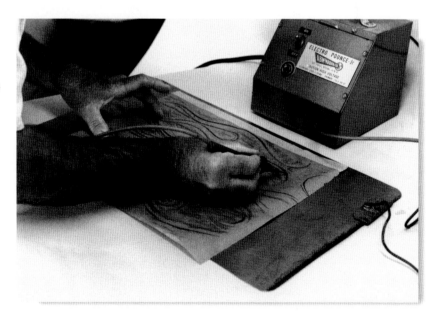

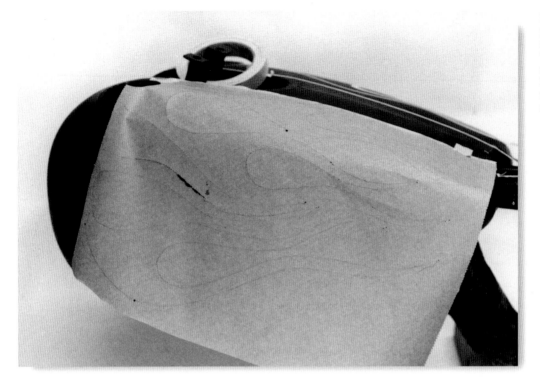

Left: This shows the pattern positioned on the opposite side of the tank. The large holes you see in the pattern were burned because I wasn't holding the paper tight enough to the piece of sheet metal.

Right: Here, I am using a pounce or chalk pad. Holding the paper tightly to the tank, I lightly pat and rub the powdered chalk through the perforations in the paper pattern.

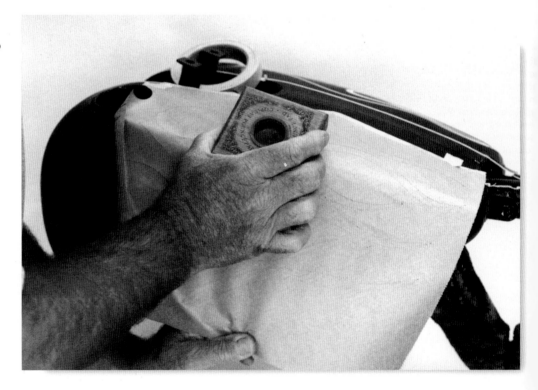

Left: Removing the pattern reveals a dotted line of chalk. Lightly blow away the excess chalk dust until there is a very faint pattern. The chalk line is fragile, so do not wipe it.

Right: The outline can now be duplicated with the 1/8-inch tape. I use this method on the fenders also and it really speeds things up.

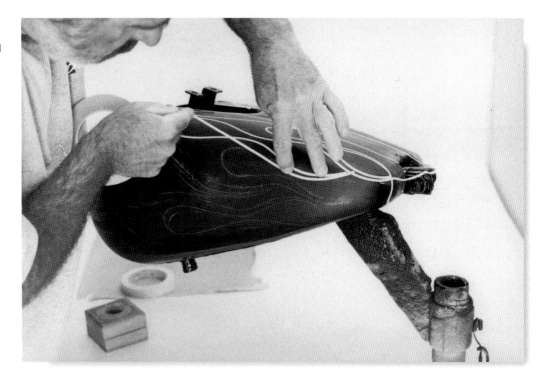

Above: When I am satisfied with the 1/8 inch outline on all the parts, I press all of the tape down firmly. Next, I wipe away any chalk dust remaining using a blower and an old, used tac rag.

Below: The next step involves applying wider tape to fill in the areas I am not going to want painted. I am using 2-inch masking tape, applied one strip at a time. The darker base allows me to see the outline through the tape. Rubbing across the design with a crayon may help but it can also contaminate subsequent coats of color if you are not careful. Using a razor blade or an X-Acto knife, I carefully cut along the center of the 1/8-inch tape impression. Be careful to only cut through the first layer of tape.

Right: Carefully pulling away the tape, I am exposing the part of the design that will painted.

Below: Pulling the tape back over itself produces a cleaner edge. Take your time with this stage. Also note the width of this first design allows room for the second set of flames.

Left: This is what all three pieces looked liked taped up ready for the first layer of flames. After checking for potential leaks in the tape and cleaning the surface with a wax and grease remover, the flames are ready to be colored.

Right: Here, I am spraying three very light and transparent coats of silver pearl mixed with clear. I wanted this to be subtle so the base color would show through. After the paint is unmasked, I then spray on three coats of urethane clear.

Above: When the clear is fully cured I sand the parts, taking care not to sand through into the color coats. As you can see in the photo, there is a ridge between the flames and the base that must be filled with more clear coats before the next design can be applied.

Right: After three or four more coats of clear, the ridge is finally smooth enough to begin the process all over again.

Above: After sanding, the tank is ready for the second set of flames. If you compare this picture to the lower photo on page 101, you can see how the ridge has been eliminated by the multiple coats of clear urethane.

Right: The second set of flames makes use of the open areas in the first pattern. I try to separate similar shapes so both designs are visible.

Above: The second set of flames is sprayed in a candy violet using toners mixed in clear. Again I am applying the coats of color lightly to allow the base and the pearl flames to show through.

Right: The next step is unmasking and cleaning all of the parts, making sure there are no paint leaks or oversprayed areas. Then I thoroughly clean the parts using a scuff pad and a sanding paste.

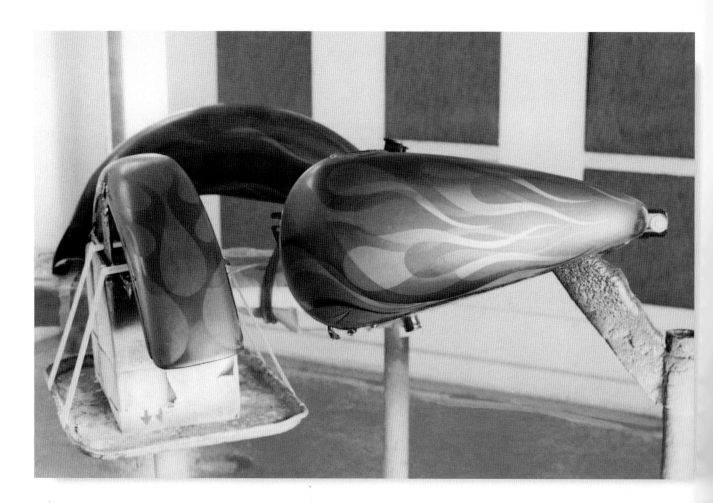

Above: Although it is not necessary with ghost flames, I outlined the last set of designs with a mixture of purple and grey striping urethane. The stripe is very subtle and sometimes almost invisible, but I feel it added extra depth to the work.

Above: It's a long and time consuming process to get to this stage, even on a motorcycle tank. The double ghost flames came out well and you can see them clearly here because of the angle at which we photgraphed them. From the front they appear to be just a light flash of color and form. The last stage is to apply the finish coats of clear urethane, sanding between every three coats until there is enough clear to allow finish rubbing. The clear coats give a lot of depth to the finish as you can see by the reflections.

Flame Folks

Von Dutch

Von Dutch flamed and striped the '51 Ford Wagon owned by George Barris and it ended up on the cover of the March 1955 issue of *Rod & Custom*. The way the cover was laid out, I thought there was going to be some information inside on how to do this kind of work but unfortunately the striping article was about an old-time craftsman, Art Summers, whose work was perfect but did not stimulate me. I was very disappointed when I found no information inside about the cover car or about Von Dutch whom, I suspected, might have done the work. Even though I lived 400 miles to the north of Los Angeles, I was beginning to hear about Von Dutch.

The first time I saw anything in a magazine about Von Dutch was the February 1956 issue of *Car Craft*. The interview was really humorous but I felt that although many of Dutch's answers contained good information, the writer was making a joke out of him. However, the pictures of his work were fascinating and I realized that it was something I wanted to try. Soon after this, his work began appearing everywhere and the custom paint craze spread to areas beyond Los Angeles.

Von Dutch's bold and colorful style made a strong visual statement as if the car was just a canvas on which to paint his ideas. When your car was "Dutched" it definitely got more attention. His work had a rebellious, irreverent appearance that was instantly a hit with the younger generation of car owners. He became so popular that soon others were imitating his work, dress and sometimes his behavior thus creating a cult that still continues today.

While Von Dutch may not have been the first person doing flames, his work was mentioned by everyone I interviewed as being influential. He did many different styles of flame designs and I believe he was the first to outline flame designs with a pinstripe. I developed my own style from Manuel Gonzales' '40 Ford pictured on the cover of the October 1956 issue of *Car Craft* although at the time I didn't know who had done the work.

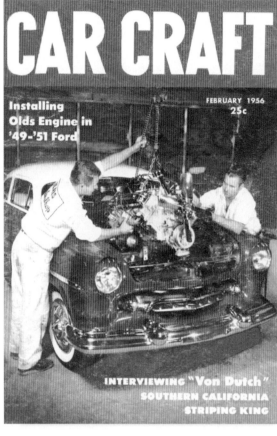

Von Dutch talked about covering grinder marks and scratches with striping thus creating a new style he labeled "Modern Pinstriping." He seems to be the guy that broke away from the regular straight line striping that was the usual form of decoration on cars since the twenties. The only time I met Von Dutch, the first thing he told me was that he didn't like to work on cars and that his real trade was as a gunsmith and machinist. He said, "I don't care if I never stripe another car!"

Left: "Von Dutch" issue of *Car Craft*: Feb, 1956.

"The biggest secret is to take your mistake and make it look like you did it on purpose. If I make a slip, I go over to the other side and do the same thing."
Car Craft, February, 1956.

"The first flying eyeball I drew was in 1947 and I haven't any idea what prompted me to even draw it then."
Car Craft, February, 1956.

"I'm good for about a year at this, then I go back to my regular job. I'm a sign writer and gun-smith by trade."
Car Craft, February, 1956.

"When Von Dutch tired of decorating cars with spiders or bloodshot eyeballs, he turned to flame jobs and they became his special trademark. Flames coming from everywhere, lapping at the body of the car from underneath, flames pouring from cowling vents in the hood, flames streaming along fenders from under the headlights, flames licking back along the roof from under the top of the windshield—the whole car being consumed by flames. As long as they were in fashion, flame jobs were the toughest to do and took the longest. But Von Dutch doesn't care. For six dollars an hour he would stripe the Queen Mary."

Roger Vaughn
"TRUE, The Man's Magazine," September, 1967.

"Dutch started it all. Everything. The painted T-shirts, pinstriping, all that crazy art work. Flying eyeballs. Flame jobs."

Ed "Big Daddy" Roth
AutoWeek, July 31,1989.

"Then came flames—Dutch again. There had been flame jobs, but not the way Dutch did 'em, just bitchin': wrap-arounds and in-and-outs and a lot of color, pinstripes around the flames. He started the T-shirt stuff, butfor himself—I don't think he ever sold them, but I did, and I did very well."

Dean Jeffries
AutoWeek, July 31, 1989

George Barris

The center of activity for many young customizers was in the shop run by George Barris in Los Angeles. I remember seeing a picture of George and his friends standing with a roadster that had flames hand-painted

n it. Since it was taken at one of the first shops George ~~d~~ in L.A., I figured he was probably doing these ~~d~~esigns before Von Dutch began striping for him. I called ~~h~~m and he confirmed it. I don't know if George was the

first ever to do this type of work, but there is a strong possibility that he was influential to Von Dutch doing his first flames. When I talked to George about early flame painting he recalled:

"The first flame painting I did was in the forties when I still lived in Northern California. The car was a '25 Buick owned by my brother Sam and me. We brush painted it a combination of designs that we called flames but were actually closer to scallops.

The first designs that began to look like what we call flames today were on a roadster and they were also done with a brush and house paint. I would study real fire trying to figure out how to get a design that would really look like it was burning. When I moved to Los Angeles and opened my own shop, at first I did the flame designs and had Von Dutch, or someone else, stripe them. Sometimes I only did the tape design or chalked it on the car to show the guys how it should look and the colors I wanted to use. A few of the flamed cars I remember doing this way were Sein's '32 coupe, Pollard's '29 roadster and my '51 Ford station wagon. The wagon became a Rod & Custom cover car after Von Dutch went wild on it when he was left alone to stripe it one night."

Dean Jeffries

Dean Jeffries' shop was next door to Barris Kustom and his wild pinstriping and paint designs soon became popular with custom car owners. Unlike Dutch, he let

Above: A rear view of Carol Lewis's Jeffries-flamed Chevy.

Above Left: The Barris-flamed, Dutch-striped Ford Woody cover of *Rod and Custom* March, 1955.

himself be photographed actually doing the work step-by-step and George Barris' articles on Jeffries were the only technical information on flame work at the time and were very helpful to many of us trying to learn. In a recent conversation Jeffries remembered:

Above: This wild bunch from sometime in the mid-fifties went on to become the best known players in their respective fields. George Barris on the left, Eddie Kuzma, Frank McGurk, Dean Jeffries and Troy Ruttman. The car failed to qualify for Indy in its two attempts but the flames sure looked good.

"Von Dutch was located just down the street from me. I don't remember seeing his work before I did my own flames but I do recall seeing the wildly flamed Mercedes gullwing he did for Earl Bruce. The first time I remember doing flames was off the ends of the short lakes pipes on a car I was pinstriping. I also flamed around the louvers on my own '47 Merc. After that, I just went crazy with striping, flames and cartoons all over it. The next car I flamed was probably the '56 Chevrolet that belonged to my girl friend at that time, Carol Lewis."

Dean brought this radically flamed '56 Chevrolet to the Monterey Kar Kapades in 1956 where I got to watch him stripe cars. He was one of my earliest influences. I had first read about him in *DIG* magazine and what impressed me most were his cartoons. I soon saw his work on other cars in magazines and car shows.

George Barris: "Jeffries did great flames."

Larry Watson

Larry Watson's work started appearing in magazines a year or so after the articles about Von Dutch and Dean Jeffries. He created many paint trends and was always coming up with new colors and designs, consequently, his paint work was soon in demand with the drive-in cruisers and show car owners. I talked with him about what had influenced his flame work:

"The first flames I saw were done by Von Dutch and Dean Jeffries. I was striping at the time and a friend named Buzzy wanted his shoebox Ford flamed. I said sure and did it (How easy he makes it sound). Next, I flamed a friend's '56 Olds. These cars were a sensation at the Clock Drive-In! A guy named Jack James saw them and brought me a brand new, black '57 Buick and wanted it flamed completely, roof, trunk, quarter panels, everything. He let me do what I wanted so I decided to get the ends of the flames an extra kick or curve. This was my all-time favorite flame job. At that time I was charging $35.00 for flames."

I believe this '57 Buick was the first "late model" to have this amount of flames. Watson's new style was very popular and many people were influenced by him and I

Above: This is some of Larry Watson's work. Note how the flames flow off the grill, headlight rings and side chrome. There are also flames done only with pinstripes in the concaved areas on the sides. The colors were all metalflakes. Larry's seaweed style of flames is quite evident on this car.

think he may have flamed more cars than anyone else at the time. Larry could do anything with paint and his results were always spectacular. He was a good looking guy with a sense of style and confidence that led him into the acting field where he was also successful. Today, I get more requests for Watson-style flames than any others.

"Watson had the best sense of style in flames and colors."

George Barris on Watson

'Larry Watson, another custom painter, is working on pearls that change color with the lighting. One pearl glows red in the sun and turns green in the shade, while another is blue in the light and gold in the dark. "Guys like to come down to my place, lock the doors and get high on the fumes of the lacquer," Watson says. "When I painted my '59, man I got so high, I went out and got a haircut, and the guy was cutting burgundy-colored hair'."

Robert H. Boyle on Watson
'The Car Cult from Rumpsville." Sports Illustrated.
April 24, 1964.

Below: John Hansen's 40 Ford flamed by Don Varner in the late fifties. You can see the hand-rubbed blends and wild pinstriping.

Don Varner

Don was the first pinstriper that let me hang around and watch him work and I have always appreciated that. He began striping when he lived in Eugene, Oregon, where he was involved with the hot rod and drag race scene. When we talked about his early paint and design influences he told me:

"I saw Von Dutch's work on the dash of a '40 Ford and I started striping after that. I don't remember where I first saw flames but they came along with doing the striping and seeing magazine articles. The first thing I flamed was a nose piece for a Stearman airplane. Then I did my Hemi-powered '56 Ford F-100 pickup; it was maroon with silver flames shaded and blended with maroon toners. The blends were hand rubbed because we didn't use clear. I used to tape the designs on the primed surface and paint one color, then I would unmask the primered area, cover the color I had just painted, and paint the next color. This way the surfaces were level and all you would feel was the stripe. I remember doing Snyder's '56 when I lived in Salinas; it was red and he wanted it flamed in blue but the color combination didn't work. A few days later, I sanded it down and repainted it in maroon with white and gold flames. It looked fine after that."

I remember watching Don mask both colors to keep the edge down and I think he started doing the painting himself because he had trouble getting other painters to do it like he wanted. I was there the day he pulled Snyder's car out of the booth with the red and blue flame job. He was right, it didn't look good. However, when he

Above: This is the '56 Ford F-100 pickup that impressed me so much when I saw it parked on the street in the 50's. Recently Don sent me this photo and I was surprised at how little I remembered about the work. The flames were much stubbier than I remembered. Pinstriping was used all over the truck to accent the work. The blends were all hand rubbed because no one was using clear coats at the time.

repainted it maroon with white and gold flames it was sensational. Sadly, that paint was only on the car about a year before it was customized again.

I always liked the way Don included extra striping in and around his flames to give the designs more interest or movement. I also liked his erotic striping and Jock Patterson's '57 Buick dashboard is one of my prized possessions. It too has flamed pinstripes in the design.

I remember him painting in the service station next to Mel's—all we could see was a big candy apple cloud of overspray. He was much more than a pinstriper and a painter, having designed some beautiful cars. As a team, Don Varner and Bill Cushenbery produced some of the best custom cars, including the Matador, Silhouette, Exodus and Marquis.

Andy Southard

Andy Southard was already well known as a custom painter and pinstriper in New York when I first met him in 1958. Not too long after that he moved to Salinas and quickly became the guy you went to if you needed striping or photography work. Andy's photo collection has been an inspiration for many years and he has always been helpful with his knowledge and many times I have called him for advice. His books on early hot rods and customs are an excellent reference about early custom painting. Recently, when I asked him about his first flame work, Andy remembered:

"I didn't do many flame paint jobs but I remember my first one was on a '40 Mercury convertible for Marty Olsen in '56. He wanted it flamed and I did it with a brush. No one showed me how to do flames, I just did them like I was striping and filled everything in with color. I had seen pictures in magazines but they didn't influence my work on this car. I learned a few things about striping when I watched Jeffries at the Monterey Kar Kapades in '56."

Many times I would have Andy outline my flames, partly because he could also photograph the car for a magazine article. His work was clean and straight and he was always willing to share his secrets.

"I was influenced by the small car books. George Sein's lime green and bronze '32 coupe was one of the first flame jobs I saw and also the '56 Chevy Jeffries did for his girlfriend, Carol Lewis. The first flames I did were on a car for Chuck Delu. In the sixties, flames came back and I was doing a lot of metalflake and blends using flame designs. Munroe's T Bucket which I painted also got a lot of attention. It was done in black with traditional yellow and orange flames."

Art is very creative in all phases of custom painting but I really like his flame work. He knows how to make the design and colors fit the car You can't go wrong with a Himsl flame job.

Above: Andy Southard flamed this '40 Mercury in the early fifties using brushes and enamel striping paint. This style of hand-painted graphic flames is coming back because of EPA regulations which have banned outdoor spray work.

Contemporary Flamers

Art Himsl

Art Himsl is known as one of today's top custom painters. His work consistently wins awards and he is one of my favorite contemporary flame artists. He was, like many of us, motivated by what he saw in the magazines.

Below: Art Himsl added gray shadows and airbrush highlights to give a 3-D effect to the flames on Andy Brizio's '32. These add to the look of the flames and shows how Art evolves his ideas constantly.

Von Franco

Franco was always a part of the car scene in Northern California and I first remember him as an airbrush artist and pinstriper doing T-shirts with people like Ed Roth and Dennis Reinero. His cars were always nostalgic-style hot rods usually in primer but his most widely known creation was his completely authentic clone of the Norm Grabowski "Kookie Kar." He now lives in the Los Angeles area where his paintings are on display in art galleries and his flames are highly visible on hot rods and customs. When I called to ask about his introduction to the phenomenon of flames he told me:

"I first saw the Kookie Kar on the TV show "77 Sunset Strip." After that, I drew pictures of hot rods with flames. I started airbrushing T-shirts in '62 and was influenced by Ed Roth. In San Jose, California, where I lived, the painters I admired were Mike Dwight and Tony Ball. My first flame job was a '50 Plymouth and I did it using house paint. One of the latest cars I have flamed is the chopped and sectioned Mercury that used to belong to Frank DeRosa. The new owner gave me complete freedom to do the job so I did a design I'd been wanting to try for quite some time. He got a great job that was different and I felt good about it."

Although he is primarily an airbrush artist, Franco does great flame designs. When he duplicated Jeffries' flames on the Kookie Kar he kept everything as close to the original as possible. He has a good sense of traditional styles and when he does do flames they really stand out.

111

Dave Bell

Dave Bell's work as a cartoonist, an artist and a pinstriper has impressed me for years. His flame style is similar to his cartoon work using a rainbow of colors and bold pinstriping. In a recent conversation about flames he recalled:

"My early flame influences were "the little books," one in particular—the Car Craft cover with the McCoy '40 sedan. Since I am not a painter, I usually do the layout and have someone else finish the job. They prep, paint, rub and clean up, then I come back and stripe."

This is a good example of using teamwork when doing flames. Dave shows how he is able to work with others to make the part he does best a lot easier.

Above: This '37 Ford sedan was done by Dave Bell and Kevin Winter in the seventies. It featured a rainbow of candy color complete with pinstriped outline that also changes color. The '37 is a fine example of Dave's work which at the time set it apart from more ordinary flame jobs.

Below: Von Franco is the artist responsible for the incredibly accurate recreation of the Norm Grabowski "Kookie Kar." Originally the flames and pinstriping were done by Jeffries and were such an important part of the original car. Franco captured it just right. This is Norm Grabowski's "Kookie Kar II." Von Franco also did the flames on the custom made hood and cowl sides. The grille is painted the body color with a "Tommy the Greek" style splash of color to match the striping on the rest of the body.

The Maestro-Aka Gerald Gaxiola Personality

This amazing cowboy artist, musician, philosopher and entertainer makes his own costumes and has incorporated the flame motif into many of them. I really love what he is doing and respect his attitude towards his art.

"Art is a religion not a business. Enlightenment is not achieved upon arrival, it is achieved along the road." He doesn't sell his work and believes: "I am afraid it will corrupt me."

Tom Prufer

Having done more flame jobs for Tom than any other car owner, I find it hard to talk about flames without Tom Prufer's name coming into the conversation. He has always provided me with a car with the right look and attitude and Tom understands the importance of stance and proportion that is so necessary to enhance the art work. His cars are real hot rods and once other car builders saw how his cars looked with flames, I began to get work from them. Many people, when they come to me for work, begin by asking for Prufer-style flames and while the flames I have done for Tom through the years are similar in color and style, each job was done on an entirely different body style car. Tom basically said, "I like what you do" and then allowed me to do it.
I do not flame every car that Tom builds but when we do work together on a project we make a good team. He has an excellent sense of what a real hot rod should be and the Prufer look, flamed or not, is usually right on as far as I am concerned.

Above: The Maestro blazes his own path and I feel my own life is richer by having met him. Photo: Tyler Hoare.

Smoothed off sterilized cars are not the Prufer style. Dropped axles, louvers, chopped tops, quick change rear ends, Halibrands, these things all combine to make the look that only Tom seems to be able to pull off. Each time he tells me, "This is my last car. I want it to be right." Maybe that's why he is able to get it right so consistently. He works as if each car is the last and keeps it simple, one car at a time.

Right: This is the famous "Cop Shop Coupe" owned and built by Tom Prufer. At first, it was just finished in black but once it was flamed it attracted a lot more attention.

This stunning pair of East Coast machines encapsulates the custom flame tradition from nose to tail. Sony Venuti's chopped '49 Mercury custom features flames which lick across the nose and down the sides. The body is finished in gloss black with a fireballed red nose with flames which roll down and around the front fenders and along the side of the car to the ends of the rear fender skirts. The '35 Ford coupe owned by Albert and Karen Chepulis features a body chopped four inches by Kelsey Martin in Beverely, Massachusetts, shaved and then fitted out with fiberglass front and rear fenders. Kelsey also painted the coupe in gloss black and detailed it out with its wildly waving flames.

Below: This sectioned '40 Ford pickup has used flames to enhance the radical bodywork. The sectioned hood sides weren't wide enough for designs so the flames appear to be coming off the front of the hood merging into the fender patterns at the upper grille corners. The bumper covers much of the lower fenders and grille so the painter chose to start the patterns higher than they might be on a non-sectioned car. I like the way the paint accents the body modifications on this car.

Above: This fenderless '34 sedan works really well with its contrasting red and blue over the solid body color. The flames run back in near scallop-style.

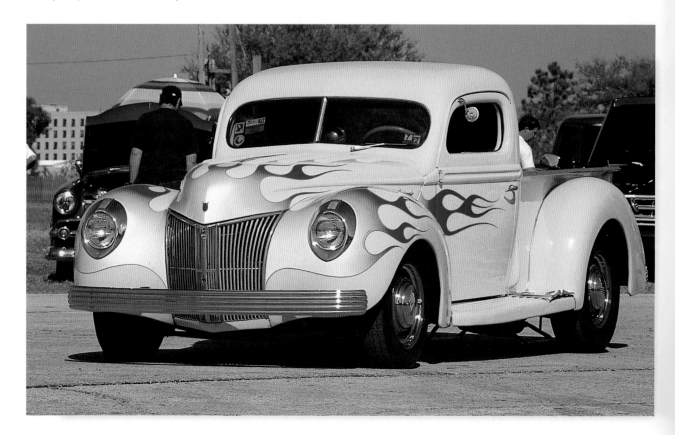

Right: The Candy Magenta flames stand out against the bright yellow base color on this radical show bike. Unusual color combinations are standard procedure with motorcycles and it is very difficult to come up with something that hasn't already been done but Arlen Ness has the talent to put it all together just right.

Left: This intricate design combines the motorcycle tank into the artwork. It mixes flames with a checkered background as it all rolls down the tank. The background and the unusual color combination are great.

ght: This double ghost flamed Sportster tank s done in shades of orange to match the ner's truck. The flames were painted in ndy orange and yellow toners with gold pearl hlights.

Below: "The Ice Cream Man From Hell" uses flame designs to draw customers to his booth at Lead East fifties party in New Jersey.

Above: Flamed apparel is quite popular today at car events and sometimes in other areas as well. This is a great looking top hat.

Right: Graffiti flames? Although this isn't on a wall, I believe it shows how today's youth uses flames as a form of expression. If Von Dutch were a kid today would he be building motorized skateboards and graffiti flaming everything in sight?

Right: Pinstriping adds a cute touch to this forty Ford. The stripe ends with a cartoon of a fireman hosing down a small fire blazing from beneath the hood.

Below: This custom '37 Ford has an original set of flames done by the late "Shakey Jake." A pearlescent white base was accented with Pagan Gold blended into candy apple red for a nostalgic effect. Scallops framing the hood louvers and the squared off designs on the lower front fenders are straight out of the late-sixties.

Left: The California Kid was the inspiration for the flames on Tom Prufer's '34 Ford Coupe. This *Rod & Custom* cover car with Manuel Reyes flames became a classic starting point for a whole new generation of flamers.

Right: Lance Blacker's '34 Ford high-boy sedan was done by Jerry Hutchinson. The flames seem to emerge from behind the grille shell and out of the hood louvers. The colors create a very nice contrast.

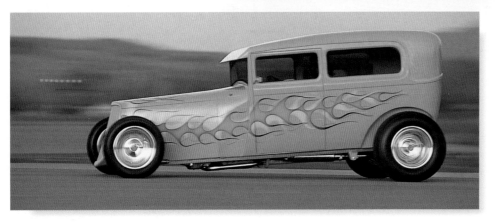

Left: Harvey Perry built his high-boy with solid hood sides that make the flames appear as if they might be blazing from the front tires. A nice job using an unusual color combination.

Above: This red and green flamed '39 Chevy is rather cool. The color combination is very different and it certainly makes the car stand out. Note how the flames flow around the grille and over the hood without hitting any lourvers. This style is not so noticeable from the front but from a 3/4-angle it jumps right up.

Left: A large mass of solid orange flares into flame patterns that stream towards the rear of the fenders and hood intertwining and overlapping as they go. The overlapped areas rely on a pinstripe to give a three dimensional effect. This doesn't require double masking when spraying but it still takes a lot thoughtful planning to make it look right.

Below: A more modern version of a '40 Ford coupe. The flames are smoother and are blended using traditional colors of yellow, orange and red. They flow rearward stopping at the cowl and windshield in a nice, well-balanced movement.

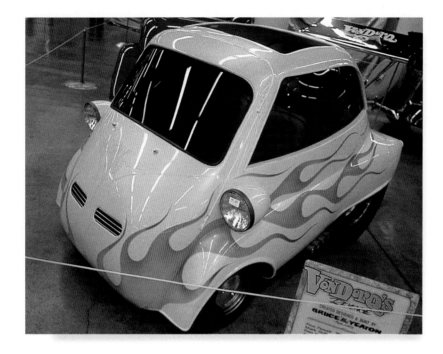

Left: This was a BMW Isetta that for years was parked behind my shop. I traded it to Bruce "Von Dorq" Yeaton for a motorized recliner he had. Bruce installed a Kawasaki motorcycle engine and proceeded to build a wild little car. The yellow pearl paint is by Mark Duliba. I laid out the tangerine flames and Alan Smith added the pinstriping.

Below: I started flaming "things" because I was getting frustrated when I was not working on cars or motorcycles. I found it was a pleasant alternative and some of the items have since been reproduced.

Above: One of the most interesting aspects of flaming is its diversity. As a form of artistic expression, flaming can be done with high-tech painting systems, aerosol cans, or four-inch brushes. The addition of temporary or permanent flames is a great way to quickly hop-up the looks of a semi-finished car. Primitive flames like the ones shown here can be done easily with the minimum of expense and are a good way to learn the basics.

Below: This mid-fifties F-100 pickup has an unusual mint green flame combination that includes the wheels, grille and interior of the truck. Note how the whitewall tires compliment the white blending in the flames. Many people think that if the paint is dull it must be primer but that is not always the case. There are additives to make many of the high tech paints of today into a matte or satin finish. Who made the rule that paint had to be glossy?

Left: Dented but still driven, this shoebox Ford looks very cool in lime green and satin primer. The flames are bold and a flowing with airbrushed edges and wide white striping. It's a simple and effective combination.

Below: Just to prove Krazy Keith can do a bit more traditional style if he has a mind to, here's a '57 Chevrolet he did recently.

Right: Mike Chase's 1951 Ford station wagon could be off of a Beach Boys' album cover. Note the flames on the top coming from behind the sun-visor.

Above: This '50 Oldsmobile looks as if it may have been stored in a time capsule for about thirty years but, in reality it was painted not too long ago by Jim Davis.

Left: The richness and blending of the candy colors and the intricate overlapping of the flames come together in an outstanding example of show-winning paint work. This '50 Mercury owned by Jim Bullman, was painted by Dick Hidalgo and flamed by Rory Pentecost.

Below: This '55 Ford looks great with single-color flame designs. Note how the patterns break into separate parts towards the rear with even the custom-made fender skirts ablaze with more flames.

Right: The brilliant colors of the flames on this early Chevelle really stand out next to the sparkle of the Rainbow Metalflake base.

Left: This is a different design that works well on this new Chevy pickup. At the front, a small scallop or flame helps to break up the large expanse of yellow with the rest of the flames becoming more traditional as they flow towards the rear quarter panel. A few more flames around the hood louvers add more color.

Opposite Page: Is this what they mean when they say "Burning Rubber"? Not everyone has a budget to carry their flaming obsessions as far as the tires do on this 1996 Dodge Sidewinder concept truck.

Right: The Bob Glembocki family has been involved in drag racing for many years. I first flamed this '69 Camaro when it was new and they were competing as the Color Me Silver racing team. Recently we repainted the same Camaro along with a twin car. The flames had to be identical and the pounce patterns definitely came in handy on these two cars.

INDEX

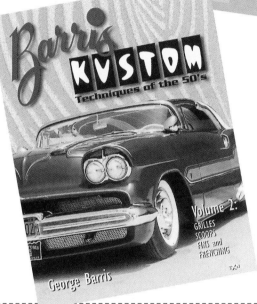
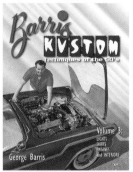